AN ACCOUNT
OF THE
ANTIQUITIES
OF THE INDIANS

A Book in the Series

Latin America

in Translation / En traducción / Em tradução

Sponsored by the Duke-University of North Carolina

Program in Latin American Studies

An Account of the
Antiquities of the Indians

FRAY RAMÓN PANÉ

A new edition with an introductory study,

notes, and appendixes by JOSÉ JUAN ARROM

Translated by SUSAN C. GRISWOLD

Chronicles of the New World Encounter

DUKE UNIVERSITY PRESS *Durham & London 1999*

Printed in the United States of America on acid-free paper ⊗

Typeset in Adobe Caslon by Tseng Information Systems

Library of Congress Cataloging-in-Publication Data appear
on the last printed page of this book.

The preparation of this work was made possible by a grant from the
National Endowment for the Humanities, an independent federal
agency. Latin America in Translation/En Traducción/Em Tradução is a
collaboration between the Duke-University of North Carolina Program
in Latin American Studies and the university presses of Duke and the
University of North Carolina. The series is supported by a grant
from the Andrew W. Mellon Foundation.

CONTENTS

ACKNOWLEDGMENTS

This book made its first appearance in Mexico in 1974, published in Spanish by Siglo XXI Editores. In 1988 I published an expanded edition, which serves as the basis for this English-language translation. To make it more accessible to an American audience, I have added an introduction that includes a short bibliography of recent works for further reading.

I incurred many debts in preparing the original Spanish-language edition. I am grateful to the Fulbright Commission and the Rockefeller Foundation, whose fellowships allowed me to take leave of my academic work during 1968 and travel to Spain to examine documents and manuscripts related to the discovery and conquest of the Antilles. In Madrid, Ramón Bela and Matilde Medina, Director and Associate Director of the Fulbright Commission, facilitated my work and offered me their cordial friendship. In New Haven, Professors Liliana and Eduard Gramberg and Ottavio di Camillo, skilled experts in the Italian and Spanish languages, kindly attended my consultations regarding the accuracy of my translation from the Italian version of Pané's manuscript.

As this new edition goes to press, I wish to acknowledge my gratitude to three distinguished Antillean scholars who have given me constant inspiration: Manuel A. García Arévalo, from the Dominican Republic, and Mercedes López-Baralt and Ricardo E. Alegría, from Puerto Rico. I would also like to express my gratitude to Professor John Jay TePaske for choosing this work as one of the first volumes in English translation of the prestigious series *Chronicles of the New World Encounter*, and to Professor Susan C. Griswold for the commendable fidelity and lucid style with which she has rendered the English translation of Pané's rather difficult text. In writing the introduction to the English edition, I have received the insuperable assistance of two Silvias, my wife Silvia Ravelo de Arrom and my daughter Silvia Marina Arrom. My thanks go to all of them.

June 1999

In the twenty-five years since I prepared the Spanish edition of Ramón Pané's *Account of the Antiquities of the Indians,* interest in the issues raised by his text has increased considerably. As the first book written on American soil in a European language, it is an important document for those who study Latin American literature. Completed around 1498, it is one of the few eyewitness accounts of the initial enounter between Spaniards and Amerindians. Based on Pané's several years of living among the native inhabitants of Hispaniola (today the island shared by Haiti and the Dominican Republic), it is the best source of information on the culture of the Taínos, as the people who greeted Columbus have come to be known.[1]

In the opening of the *Account,* Pané declared that he was "a humble friar" sent by Christopher Columbus to live among the natives to report on whatever he might "discover and understand of the beliefs and idolatries of the Indians." His report fulfilled Columbus's mandate but also went much further. In addition to recording the Taínos' myths and religious ceremonies, Pané described some of their language and daily cus-

---

1. Many of the names of the indigenous peoples of the Americas (beginning with the term Indian) are European constructs. The term *Taíno* for the native inhabitants of the Greater Antilles and some smaller islands is based on the word that both Columbus and Dr. Diego Alvarez Chanca (a physician who traveled on the second voyage) reported that the natives used when differentiating themselves from the Caribs. For the evolution of the term, which is widely used in Spanish, French, Italian, English, and other European languages, see Ricardo E. Alegría, "El uso de la terminología etno-histórica para designar las culturas aborígenes de las Antillas," *Cuadernos Prehispánicos* (Valladolid, 1981), pp. 3–29; and Irving Rouse, *The Taínos: Rise and Decline of the People Who Greeted Columbus* (New Haven, 1992). The Taíno language refers to what Columbus called the "universal language" of Hispaniola, one of many languages in what we now term the Arawak family. On the other languages of the region, see Douglas M. Taylor, *Languages of the West Indies* (Baltimore, 1977).

toms. He related details of the evangelization of Hispaniola as well as of the natives' resistance to the Spanish colonization. In a dramatic scene culminating in the murder of some of the first converts, he revealed the conflicts among the indigenous people about how to deal with the Spaniards. Our "humble friar" thus produced a document of great value to anthropologists, historians, linguists, and literary critics, as well as to the general reader interested in this pivotal moment of the American past.

By the middle of the sixteenth century the Taíno world had largely vanished from the Spanish Antilles, victim to the Conquest and the European diseases that decimated the native population. Numerous Taíno words have survived, such as *huracán, canoa, hamaca,* and *barbacoa* borrowed by Spaniards to describe the unfamiliar hurricanes, canoes, hammocks, and outdoor cooking method that they first encountered on Hispaniola.[2] The new colonial society assimilated such Taíno customs as the smoking of tobacco, the construction of palm-thatched dwellings (*bohíos*), and the preparation of the staple food *yuca,* better known to us as *cassava* or (in a processed form) tapioca. The many Taíno women who married Spaniards passed part of their culture on to their *mestizo* children. A few Taíno communities survived in isolated areas, as did others close to the Spanish settlements, designated by the new authorities as *pueblos de indios,* or Indian villages.[3] Yet the Taíno society as such had disappeared.

Luckily, Pané preserved some of their culture for posterity. Although we cannot know how well he understood what he heard, Pané appears to have been an attentive listener. His commission from Columbus required him to record the Taínos' beliefs and ceremonies as accurately as possible. Much of what he reported has since been corroborated by artifacts discovered in the Dominican Republic, Haiti, Cuba, Puerto Rico, and Jamaica. These include numerous *zemis* (religious images) with the physical characteristics of the gods in the myths he recounted, as well as the bifurcated inhalers for the hallucinogen *cohoba* (not the same as tobacco) that he described. In addition, some of the myths he recounted bear strong resemblances to the Amazonian myths of the Taínos' South American relatives, further proof of the reliability of his

2. The best dictionary to document Taíno word survivals remains Alfredo Zayas y Alfonso, *Lexicografía Antillana* (Havana, 1914). See also José J. Arrom, *Estudios de lexicología Antillana* (Havana, 1980).

3. Some of the *pueblos de indios* frequently referred to in seventeenth-century documents include Guanabacoa, next to the city of Havana, and others near Bayamo, Santiago, and Guantánamo, Cuba. See, for example, Felipe Pichardo Moya, *Los aborígenes de las Antillas* (Mexico City, 1956).

account.[4] Nonetheless, some Taíno concepts may have been distorted as they were translated into Spanish and, for this edition, retranslated into English. For example, the term "heaven" in the second paragraph of the current edition was originally "cielo," by which Pané may only have meant "sky" rather than the Christian heaven.

Of course, unlike a modern ethnographer, Pané's goal was to convert the Taínos to Christianity. A fervent missionary, he labeled them "heathen" and "idolaters." Yet he was respectful enough of their culture so that when he described the healing rituals of their priests, or *behiques*, he called them "physicians" rather than "sorcerers" or "charlatans." Indeed, he appears to have developed a sympathetic relationship with the people among whom he lived, for his *Account* repeated their complaints against the Spaniards, who "were wicked and had taken possession of their lands by force." This criticism of his countrymen makes Fray Ramón the first of many priests to expose the abuses committed against the Indians by the new settlers, proof of the complicated nature of Spanish colonialism, which contained several contradictory tendencies. For the desires to acquire land, wealth, and power, to spread Christianity, and to create a utopia in what Europeans considered a new world coexisted in the colonial enterprise, thus pitting the Church, the Crown, and the settlers against each other.[5]

Ramón Pané remains an obscure figure. In the twenty-five years since I edited his *Account*, little new biographical information has become available. We still do not know when he was born or when he died, only that he came from the Spanish region of Catalonia, where he entered the priesthood as a "humble friar of the Order of Saint Jerome." In 1992, on the occasion of presenting the translation of my edition into his native Catalan language, I was able to confirm my original hypothesis about the date when he traveled to America. When I visited the Convent of San Jerónimo de la Murtra in Badalona, near Barcelona, I was told that Pané was a young brother there when the "Catholic Kings," Ferdinand and Isabela, received Columbus in that convent on his triumphal return to Spain in 1493. Inspired by the astonishing news of Columbus's first voyage beyond the Atlantic, Pané joined the second expedition and sailed

4. Some Taíno myths also resemble those of Europe, a suggestion of the universality of myth. I have studied the Taíno myths and reproduce images of numerous *zemis* and ceremonial objects in my book *Mitología y artes prehispánicas de las Antillas* (Mexico City, 1975; rev. 2d edition 1989). For excellent reproductions of these objects, see *Taíno: Pre-Columbian Art and Culture from the Caribbean*, ed. Fátima Bercht, Estrellita Brodsky, John Alan Farmer, and Dicey Taylor (New York, 1998).
5. See Charles Gibson, *Spain in America* (New York, 1966).

for the Caribbean on September 25, 1493. By early 1494 he had settled on the north of the island in the province of the *cacique* (Indian chief) Mayobanex. In the spring of 1495, following Columbus's instructions, he moved on to the land of Guarionex, where he lived for several years. There, with the help of a native interpreter, he learned the "universal language" spoken in Hispaniola and wrote his *Account*. After he gave Columbus his manuscript, probably in 1498, we lose all trace of the friar, who "wore himself out in order to learn all this."

The fate of Pané's *Account* after that is still shrouded in mystery. The long-lost original manuscript has not yet appeared. The full text survives only because Columbus's son Fernando included it in the biography he wrote in defense of his father, who had fallen into disfavor with the Spanish monarchs. Because of a hostile political climate in Spain, Fernando was unable to publish his *History of the Admiral don Cristopher Columbus by his son don Fernando* during his lifetime. It is only known in Alfonso de Ulloa's poor Italian translation of 1571, on which I have based my edition. Because of the many inaccuracies of Ulloa's transcriptions of Taíno words, which I explain in the introductory study, I compared them with those given by three of Pané's contemporaries and used these to try to determine the original Taíno terms.

I originally included appendixes of the relevant excerpts of these works as an aid to scholars who wished to check the references from my footnotes in context. I now realize that the appendixes will also be of value to the general reader. As the earliest European writings on the beliefs and customs of the inhabitants of the New World, they reflect the learning process that Europeans underwent as they began to understand the culture of the Taínos. Appendix A reproduces three selections from the writings of Christopher Columbus. The last excerpt, written after he became familiar with the friar's investigations, shows how the Admiral changed his initial mistaken impression, revealed in the first two selections, that the Taínos had no religion. The other two appendixes reproduce selections from the works of two men who handled Pané's manuscript and used it as the source for some of the information they provided on the inhabitants of the Antilles. Appendix B is by Pietro Martire d'Anghiera, also known in English as Peter Martyr. An Italian humanist who served in the Spanish court, he paraphrased parts of the *Account* in his own book on the discovery and colonization of America, a collection of letters he wrote from 1494 on and published in Latin in 1516 as the *Decades of the New World*. Although his information was secondhand, since he never set foot in America, it was one of the earliest reports on Spain's new possessions widely diffused throughout Europe. Appendix C, by Fray Bartolomé de las Casas, shows how much more

Europeans knew by the middle of the sixteenth century. Las Casas, the great "Defender of the Indians," wrote three histories of the Spanish conquest of the Caribbean. In his *Apologetic History of the Indies*, finished near the end of his life in 1566, he used Pané's *Account* to supplement what he himself had seen in Hispaniola and Cuba, where he had lived intermittently between 1502 and 1547, first as a settler and then as a priest who mounted a vigorous critique of Spanish colonialism. In addition to documenting the changing state of European knowledge about native Americans, these appendixes reveal the difficulties of studying long-lost texts as well as those of understanding long-lost cultures.

For those who wish to explore these issues further, I recommend the following works. For the most complete study of the Taínos, see Irving Rouse, *The Taínos: Rise and Decline of the People Who Greeted Columbus* (New Haven, 1992). For the most recent, see Fátima Bercht, Estrellita Brodsky, John Alan Farmer, and Dicey Taylor, eds., *Taíno: Pre-Columbian Art and Culture From the Caribbean* (New York, 1998). On the myths of the Taínos, see José Juan Arrom, *Mitología y artes prehispánicas de las Antillas* (Mexico City, 1975; rev. 2d ed. 1989), which expands on this study of Pané's *Account*. An excellent collection of articles by several authors on the indigenous peoples of the Caribbean, with an up-to-date bibliography, is Samuel M. Wilson, ed., *The Indigenous People of the Caribbean* (Gainesville, Fla., 1997). For recent approaches to the encounter between Europeans and Amerindians, see especially Alfred W. Crosby, Jr., *The Columbian Exchange: Biological and Cultural Consequences of 1492* (Westport, Conn., 1972); Peter Hulme, *Colonial Encounters: Europe and the Native Caribbean, 1492–1797* (London, 1986); Peter Hulme and Neil Whitehead, eds., *Wild Majesty: Encounters with Caribs from Columbus to the Present Day* (Oxford, 1992); and Stuart Schwartz, *Implicit Understandings: Observing, Reporting, and Reflecting on the Encounters between Europeans and Other Peoples in the Early Modern Era* (Cambridge, 1994).

With regard to the notes, when the changes have consisted of a slight retouching, they have been added without altering the number of the note; when the additions have constituted a major contribution, however, they have been incorporated in a separate paragraph and indicated by the addition of the letter *a* to the corresponding number. Likewise, I have thought it would be more convenient to move the notes to the bottom of the page to eliminate for the reader the annoyance of having to flip between the text and the endnotes.

When their source is not indicated, the quotations from Pietro Martire d'Anghiera and from Bartolomé de Las Casas included in the footnotes are to be found in their respective sections in appendixes B and C.

INTRODUCTORY STUDY

Ramón Pané's *Account of the Antiquities of the Indians* constitutes a watershed in the cultural history of the Americas. Written on the island of Hispaniola during the early days of the Conquest, the *Account* is the only surviving direct source of information about the myths and ceremonies of the first inhabitants of the Antilles. Because it was completed about 1498, it is the first book written on American soil in a European language. And because Fray Ramón was also the first missionary who learned the language and studied the beliefs of an indigenous people, his *Account* is likewise a fundamental text in ethnological studies in this hemisphere.[1]

1. Pané's primacy in this and other disciplines is now being recognized in ever wider circles. At the end of the nineteenth century, Count de la Viñaza pointed out that "Román Pané [*sic*] . . . was the first European who was particularly known to speak an American language" (*Bibliografía española de las lenguas indígenas de América* [Madrid, 1892], p. 10). In 1906, Edward Gaylor Bourne, a professor at Yale University, translated the text into English and declared that "[Fray] Ramón's report of his observations and inquiries is not only the first treatise ever written in the field of American antiquities, but to this day remains our most authentic record of the religion and folklore of the long since extinct tainos" (*Columbus, Ramon Pane and the Beginnings of American Anthropology* [Worcester, 1906], published also in *Proceedings of the American Antiquarian Society*, New Series 17 [1906]: 310–84). In 1920, the German missionary Robert Streit declared that "the Hieronymite friar indeed deserves the honor of the title of first ethnographer of America" ("Fr. Roman Panes O.S. Hier, der erste Ethnograph Amerikas," *Zeitschrift für Missionswissenschaft* 10 [1920]: 192–93). In 1945, Max Henríquez Ureña, member of a family of distinguished educators, called him "the first teacher of the Indians" (*Panorama de la literatura dominicana* [Rio de Janeiro, 1945], p. 11). In 1950, Father Constantino Bayle said that to Pané "belongs the glory of first catechist, first missionary and first ethnologist of America" (*El clero secular y la evangelización de América* [Madrid, 1950], p. 42). Rodolfo Barón Castro, who has made a considerable contribution in making known Fray Ramón's importance beyond the limited circles of specialists, characterizes him as "initiator of literacy in the New

Pané's report is thus a classic text in American anthropology. As reporter, he noted down the names, functions, and attributes of the Taíno gods, and he recounted the aboriginal people's beliefs about what became of their souls after death. He described the ceremonies of the priests, or *behiques*, and the cures they performed. He collected the myths they told him about the origin of the sun and the moon, the creation of the sea and the fishes, the appearance of man on the island, and the cultivation and consumption of cassava. He related some details of the evangelization of Hispaniola and explained the meaning of several Taíno words. He even related the melancholy prophecy, pronounced by an aged *cacique* (chieftain), that clothed people were to arrive who would lay waste his lands and kill his unhappy descendants.

It is understandable that the document has aroused great interest throughout the nearly five centuries since its composition and that there are numerous versions of it in the principal European languages. These versions, however, have been unsatisfactory for various reasons, and because of the adverse circumstances I describe below, they have given rise to inaccuracies that impair the studies based on them. It seems, then, that a clarification of the difficulties of the text is needed, as well as a reliable edition easily accessible to scholars who wish to pursue the historical, linguistic, and ethnographic questions suggested by this unique document.

Let us begin by establishing the chronology of the work. In the opening of the *Account*, Pané declares that he is "a humble friar of the Order of Saint Jerome" who went by order of Columbus to live among the indigenous people so as to report to him whatever he might have been able to "discover and understand about the beliefs and idolatries of the Indians." Fray Bartolomé de Las Casas, who was personally acquainted with our friar, attested that he "came to this island at the beginning with the Admiral."[2] Pané, however, could not have accompanied the admiral on the first journey because the crew members who stayed behind in the Navidad fort in 1492 are known to have been killed within a few months by Chief Caonabó and his people. According to Pané's own account, by 1496 he had already spent two years in his evangelizing work on His-

World" (Oficina de Educación Iberoamericana, *Aspectos de la alfabetización en Iberoamérica* [Madrid, 1966], pp. 201-6). Germán Arciniegas has published an informative article on Pané that he entitled, "Our First Anthropologist" (*Americas* 23, nos. 11 and 12 [November-December 1971]: 2-10).

2. Fray Bartolomé de Las Casas, *Apologética historia de las Indias*, chap. 120; in the Madrid, 1909, edition, p. 322.

paniola. We may assume, then, that he arrived in 1494, on the second voyage. We do not have a complete list of the passengers on this voyage,[3] but it has been established that they comprised between twelve hundred and fifteen hundred individuals; among them were a few priests, the majority of whom had been recruited in Catalonia, Pané's homeland. Because the exact dates of that journey are known, we can assume that Fray Ramón left Cadiz on September 25, 1493, reached Navidad on November 28 of the same year, continued on board while a site was being selected to found the new colony, and disembarked in Isabela on January 2, 1494.[4]

Once in Hispaniola, Fray Ramón tells us he went on "to the Magdalena, a fortress built by Don Christopher Columbus," in which fortress he remained "in the company of Artiaga, its commander." While he was at the fortress, "the said Admiral arrived to relieve Artiaga and some Christians under siege by the enemy, subjects of a principal *cacique* called Caonabó" (*Account*, chap. XXV). The rebellion of the indigenous people and Columbus's arrival at the Magdalena can also be dated with some certainty. In the company of his brother Bartolomé and of Alonso de Hojeda, the admiral left the settlement of Isabela at the head of a strong column on March 24, 1495; two days later he and his people did battle with the *cacique* Guatiguaná, whose hosts they defeated in Puerto de los Hidalgos; from there, they went on to relieve Magdalena.[5] Columbus's arrival at the fortress thus must have been toward the end of March 1495. By that time, Fray Ramón had been on the island for more than a year and, we may assume, had learned the Macorís language.

From his interview with Columbus on that occasion and from the journey he undertook subsequently, Fray Ramón relates the following:

> The Lord Admiral told me then that the language spoken in the province of Magdalena [or] Macorís was different from the other one and was not understood throughout the country. Rather, I should go to live with another principal *cacique* called Guarionex, lord of many people because his language was understood throughout the land. Thus, by his command, I went to live with the said Guarionex. And it is indeed true that I said to the Lord Governor

3. Regarding this second voyage, Samuel Eliot Morison, who has studied the voyages of Columbus in detail, says: "The payrolls and crew lists have never been found, and we know the names of very few of the men" (*Admiral of the Ocean Sea, A Life of Christopher Columbus* [Boston, 1944], p. 395).
4. Ibid., pp. 398–428.
5. Ibid., pp. 488–90; also Las Casas, *Historia de las Indias*, book 1, chaps. 14 and 15.

Map 1. The modern Caribbean. After Irving Rouse, *Migrations in Prehistory: Inferring Population Movement from Cultural Remains* (New Haven: Yale University Press, 1986), fig. 21.

Christopher Columbus: "Sir, how is it that Your Lordship wishes me to go to live with Guarionex, knowing no language other than that of Macorís? Let Your Lordship grant leave for some of the Nuhuirey people, who later became Christians and knew both languages, to accompany me." He granted this request and told me to take with me whoever pleased me. And God in his goodness gave me for company the best of the Indians. . . . he was Guatícabanú, who afterwards became a Christian and was called Juan. . . .

Guatícabanú and I left and went to Isabela, and there we waited for the Lord Admiral until he returned from lifting the siege of the Magdalena. And as soon as he arrived, we went to where the Lord Governor had sent us, in the company of a man by the name of Juan de Ayala, who was in charge of a fortress the said Governor Christopher Columbus had ordered built a half league from the place where we were to reside . . . which fortress was called La Concepción. Consequently we were with that *cacique* Guarionex almost two years. (*Account*, chap. XXV)

The details Pané gives here about the fortresses and their commanders coincide exactly with the information gathered by Las Casas.[6] And

6. Las Casas, *Historia de las Indias,* book 1, chap. 110; in the Mexico City, 1951, edition, vol. 1, p. 429.

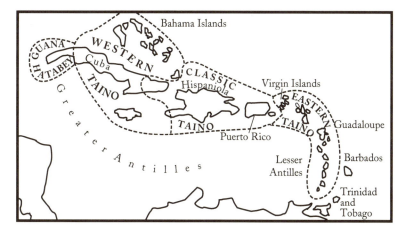

Map 2. Location of cultures in the West Indies when Columbus arrived. After Irving Rouse, *The Tainos: Rise and Decline of the People Who Greeted Columbus* (New Haven: Yale University Press, 1992), p. 8.

as far as the chronology is concerned, its validity is corroborated by the other details. If Fray Ramón reached Guarionex's territory in the spring of 1495, the "almost two years" he spent there would take us to the end of 1496. In effect, he tells us: "Seeing that Guarionex was retreating and abandoning what we had taught him, we decided to leave and to go where we might gather better fruit. . . . And thus we went to another principal *cacique* who showed us good will, saying he wanted to be a Christian. This *cacique* was called Mabiatué" (*Account,* chap. XXV). The approximate date of this journey can be established because of an unfortunate episode. On the second day after Fray Ramón's departure, six of Guarionex's subjects took some images the friar had left behind and buried them in a plot of ground as they were in the habit of doing with some of their own idols so that the earth might bear better fruits. But because the newly arrived Spaniards did not understand the nature of such propitiatory rituals, they thought the islanders wished to mock the images. Pané adds: the "elders . . . ran shouting to inform Don Bartolomé Columbus, who had been entrusted with that government by the Admiral his brother, who had gone to Castile. The former, as the deputy of the Viceroy and Governor of the islands, brought the wrongdoers to trial, and when the truth was known, he had them publicly burned" (*Account,* chap. XXVI). Columbus is known to have left for Castile in March 1496, leaving the governorship in his brother's hands until he returned in August 1498.[7] The date of Pané's departure from the lands of Guarionex, toward the end of 1496, thus coincides with Columbus's absence.

Here arises a doubt that is difficult to resolve regarding both the form and the time frame of Pané's report to Columbus. It must have been during his stay in Guarionex's territory—between the spring of 1495 and the spring of 1496—that Pané gathered the information on the Taínos' beliefs that he recorded in the first twenty-one of the twenty-six chapters of the *Account*. Did he deliver those twenty-one chapters to Columbus before Columbus departed on his return voyage in March 1496? Or did he orally inform him of the results of his research up to that point, finishing the written *Account* years later? We know, at least, that the deplorable episode of the buried images occurred after the admiral's departure. In chapter XXVI, Fray Ramón specifies that "the first who received holy baptism on the Island of Hispaniola was Juan Mateo, who was baptized on the day of the Evangelist Saint Matthew in the year of 1496." Saint Matthew's day falls on the twenty-first of September, so the baptism was also carried out after Columbus had left. Furthermore, Fray Ramón relates subsequent events that extend beyond this last date, September 21, 1496. That Juan Mateo, who was then baptized, is the same man of whom he said previously: "God in his goodness gave me for company the best of the Indians. . . . He was Guaticabanu, who afterwards became a Christian and was called Juan." In explaining the circumstances of Guaticabanu's death, he comments: "The first to be killed and to receive the baptismal water, was an Indian named Guatícaba,[8] who later took the name of Juan. . . . And in this manner his brother Antón died as well, and with him another. . . . Those who remained alive and are still living today are Christians . . . and now by the grace of God there are many more Christians" (chap. XXV). If others survived who "are still living today" and there were later "many more Christians," it is clear that the last chapters of the *Account* were completed after the baptism was carried out on September 21, 1496. This internal evidence would support the hypothesis that when Columbus undertook his return journey to Spain, he was acquainted with the results of Fray Ramón's research but had not yet received the manuscript of the *Account*. Some external evidence tends to reinforce the same hypothesis. In letters dated between June 13, 1497, and May 12, 1499, Pietro Martire d'Anghiera makes reference to

7. Morison, *Admiral*, pp. 497 and 564.
8. *Gua-[t]í-ca-ba-nu* and *Gua-tí-ca-ba-[nu]*, with the missing letters supplied in brackets, are the same name.

Map 3. Island of Hispaniola (modern Haiti/Dominican Republic) at the time of Columbus, with ancient place names and home villages of Hispaniolan chiefs indicated by dots. After Irving Rouse, *The Tainos: Rise and Decline of the People Who Greeted Columbus* (New Haven: Yale University Press, 1992), p. 144.

some of the myths Pané collected,[9] but his references are scattered, imprecise, and incomplete. In none of the letters does he mention a written source, and, indeed, in the last one he indicates that he has been reporting "what recently they have told me about them."[10] One may thus surmise that Anghiera was merely relating to his Italian friends some random details gleaned from his conversations with the admiral.

One more piece of internal evidence helps us establish the chronology. In concluding his story, Pané once again mentions *cacique* Mabiatué —whom he now calls Mahubiatívire[11] and "who has continued to be of good will for three years now, saying he wishes to be a Christian" (chap. XXVI). This *cacique* had expressed his desire to be a Christian between 1495 and 1496, so the three additional years take us up to the end of 1498.

The record of Pané's travels in Hispaniola allows us to clarify two questions of considerable importance. In the first place, it is clear that the *Account* was not completed in 1496, as has been commonly believed.[12]

9. Pietro Martire d'Anghiera, *Epistolario,* study and translation by José López de Toro, 3 vols. [Madrid, 1953-1955]. The letters referred to are numbered 177, 180, 189, 190, and 206, and they appear in volume 1, pp. 335-36, 340-41, 356-58, 361-62, and 390, respectively.
10. Ibid., p. 390.
11. *Ma-hu-bia-tí-ui-re* and *Ma-[hu]-bia-t[i]-ue-[re],* with the missing letters supplied in brackets, are the same name.
12. See, for example, the edition entitled *Relación de Indias 1496,* with a prologue and notes by Alberto Wildner-Fox (Buenos Aires, 1954).

The evidence cited above indicates that it was completed after 1496 and no earlier than 1498. In the second place, the record of Pané's travels tends to resolve the doubts cast on his linguistic competence and consequently on his credibility as a reliable reporter. Fernando Ortiz has objected that our friar, "according to Las Casas, understood only one of the three languages of the Indians of Quisqueya, that of the lower Macorixes, which was not the general language of the island."[13] Pedro Henríquez Ureña, agreeing with Ortiz, declares that "the language Pané spoke was not Taíno, the general language of the island, but lower Macorix: see Las Casas, *Apologética historia de las Indias*, Chapter 120."[14] Let us consider precisely what Las Casas says in the cited chapter: "This Fray Ramón found out what he could, insofar as he understood the languages, for there were three spoken on this island; he knew only one, however, that of a small province that we said above was called lower Macorix, and he knew that language only imperfectly. *Of the universal language he knew very little, like the rest of the Spaniards, although more than the others* because no one—neither clergyman, friar, nor layman— knew any of them perfectly except for a sailor from Palos or from Moguer who was called Cristóbal Rodríguez." In light of the chronology previously established, one can now give Las Casas's testimony and specifically the italicized section a less negative interpretation. As we have seen, Fray Ramón lived several years among the Taínos, and he had time, particularly with the support and assistance of Guaticabanu, to learn something of the new language and to obtain the information he wanted.

The trajectory of the manuscript after 1498 has been even more difficult to determine. Columbus returned to Hispaniola in August 1498 and remained there until August 1500,[15] so one may suppose that Fray Ramón would have hastened to finish his report in order to deliver it to the admiral then. In that case, it would have been the admiral himself who took it to Spain on his return from the third voyage. This conjecture agrees with the fact that although he does not mention the existence of a manuscript before 1499, Anghiera does give evidence that he handled the manuscript between 1500 and 1504. In fact, the strange document so awakened his interest that he included it—this time explicitly indicating its source and including several Taíno names—in an extensive letter in Latin directed to Cardinal Ludovico de Aragón. The letter became

13. Fernando Ortiz, in the prologue to Lewis Hanke, *Bartolomé de Las Casas: Pensador político, historiador, antropólogo* (Havana, 1949), p. xix.
14. Pedro Henríquez Ureña, "La cultura y las letras coloniales en Santo Domingo," in *Obra crítica* (Mexico, 1960), p. 384.
15. Morison, *Admiral*, p. 571.

part of the *Década primera* (book 9, chaps. 4–7). An Italian translation of that *Década* published in 1504[16] confirms that Anghiera had seen the manuscript in Spain before that date.

Fray Bartolomé de Las Casas also saw the manuscript in Spain. Driven by the noble effort to gather whatever information might serve in his defense of the humanity of the Indian, he extracted from the *Account* the information about Taíno beliefs that he gives in chapters 120, 166, and 167 of his *Apologética historia de las Indias*.

The *Account* was also included, in its totality, in chapter 61 of the *Historia del almirante don Cristóbal Colón por su hijo don Fernando*. Fernando's work, written in Spanish, was still unpublished when he died in 1539. Alfonso de Ulloa translated it into Italian, and this version was published in Venice in 1571.[17] But after that date, nothing further has been heard of either Pané's manuscript or Fernando's.[18] As a result, all we know of the *Account* at present is Anghiera's summary in Latin, Las Casas's extract in Spanish, and Ulloa's Italian translation.

Had Ulloa's translation been a model of precision, many of the difficulties that obscure the *Account* would have been avoided, but this was not the case. Ulloa did not live to complete the translation properly. What he left was an incomplete draft that friends published after his death in a Venetian jail in 1570.[19] Lacunae remain, as can be seen in the text—gaps that the translator may have intended to fill in a final revision he was not able to finish. In addition, numerous errors and incongruencies might be resolved if one could compare the translation with

16. Although the Latin edition of the *Década primera* was published in Seville in 1511, an Italian translation was published previously: *Libretto di tutta la navegazione dei rei di Spagna delle isole e terreni nuovamente trovati* (Venice, 1504).

17. *Historie del S.D. Fernando Colombo; nelle quali s'ha particolare & vera relatione della vita & de'fatti dell'Ammiraglio D. Christoforo Colombo, suo padre. . . . Nuouamente di lingua spagnola tradotte nell'italiana dal S. Alfonso Vlloa* (Venice, 1571).

18. Because of the loss of Fernando's manuscript, the authenticity of the work translated by Ulloa came to be questioned in the nineteenth century. For this reason, some believed that it was a fraud perpetrated by Ulloa, and others that it was the work of Pérez de Oliva or perhaps of Las Casas himself. The matter has been resolved by the discovery of a copy of Pérez de Oliva's manuscript. I have published this document, with an introductory study and notes: Bogotá, 1965; there is now a new edition, with modernized text and updated footnotes, Mexico City, 1991.

19. Regarding the causes of Ulloa's imprisonment and the circumstances of his death, unknown until a few years ago, see Othón Arróniz, "Alfonso de Ulloa, servidor de don Juan Hurtado de Mendoza," *Bulletin Hispanique* 70, nos. 3–4 (1968): 437–57, and also Antonio Rumeu de Armas, *Hernando Colón, historiador del descubrimiento de América* (Madrid, 1973), pp. 371–75.

the Spanish original. Beyond these inaccuracies, which can be remedied at times by a careful reading, Ulloa created a new source of confusion when he chose to give an Italian version of many of the names in the *Account*. The forts of Magdalena and Concepción he calls "Maddalena" and "Concettione," but his translation of the names in this case does not cause any particular difficulty. When he calls Juan de Ayala, the commander of the second fort, "Giovanni di Agiada," however, the Italianization of the last name can lead and in fact has led to some confusion: in more than one version, the name appears retranslated as "Juan de Aguado."

A similar fate has befallen the very name of the author. The title of the Italian version begins thus: "Scrittura di fra Roman delle antichità de gl'indiani." The first paragraph of the text begins: "Io, frate Roman, povero eremita." Throughout the report, Ulloa continues to write "Roman" (with one exception, chapter XXV bis, in which he calls him "Romano"). In chapter XXV bis and subsequently in the colophon, the complete name is written "Roman Pane." Several authors, following Ulloa, have simply accentuated the first name and call Pané "Román." But was he "Román"? In identifying the source of his information, Anghiera writes "fratis Ramoni."[20] Las Casas mentions Pané in the *Apologética*, declaring: "The Admiral . . . had sent a Catalan who had taken a friar's habit, and they called him Fray Ramón." And again: "There were also on this island two friars of St. Francis, laymen, although good men, whom I met as I had met Fray Ramón."[21] Because Anghiera, who had the documents at hand, translates "Ramoni," and Las Casas, who knew Pané, calls him "Ramón," it must have been Ramón and not Román.

The friar's last name has also suffered some confusion. Many scholars, following Ulloa, write it as a paroxytone: "Pane." Rinaldo Caddeo, thinking that the name would have been "Pan," remarks: "Ramon Pan e non Roman Pane scrisse forse D. Fernando."[22] If one considers the Catalan origin of our friar, however, it seems appropriate to suppose that in fact the name would have been an oxytone: Pané, like Barraqué, Bisbé, Farré, Marcané, Marcé, Mercadé, or Parladé—all names of Antillean families of Catalan origin.

If such slips occurred with Spanish Christian and family names, the reader may imagine what mischief has beset the Taíno names and terms

20. I cite from the edition of Alcalá de Henares, 1516, unnumbered folio 21.

21. Las Casas, *Apologética historia de las Indias*, chap. 120; in the cited edition, pp. 321 and 322.

22. Rinaldo Caddeo, ed., *Le historie della vita e dei fatti di Cristoforo Colombo per D. Fernando Colombo suo figlio*, 2 vols. (Milan, 1930), 2:33, note 8.

in the *Account*. These words, polysyllabic and totally alien to European scribes and publishers, lent themselves in successive transcriptions to the confusion of some letters and the omission of others. The double process of mistakes and violent Italianizations has affected them all in one way or another. Among the names already mentioned, the toponym Macorix appears as "Maroris," the anthroponym Caonabó as "Caouabo," and poor Juan Mateo sometimes is called "Guaicabanú" and others "Guatícaba." In the same fashion, *conucos* (small farms) are called "conichi" in an italianized plural, *jobos* (hog plum trees) are called "iobi," and *yuca* (cassava or manioc) is at times called "giuca" and at others "giutola." The names of gods and cultural heroes have suffered the greatest distortion, as can be imagined. The name of one of them, Bayamanaco, appears transcribed in four different ways: Bassamanaco, Aiamauaco, Baiamanicoel, and Gamanacoel.

To these difficulties one must add the fact that the original *Account* suffered from a certain degree of disorganization and confusion. Fray Ramón himself warns in chapter V: "And because they have neither writing nor letters, they cannot give a good account of how they have heard this from their ancestors, and therefore they do not all say the same thing, nor can one write down in an orderly fashion what they tell." In the following chapter, he repeats the complaint and adds: "Therefore, I believe that I put first what ought to be last and the last first." In chapter VIII, accepting some of the blame himself, Pané declares: "Because I wrote it down in haste and did not have sufficient paper, I was not able to write down in that place what I had copied down elsewhere by mistake." And realizing at times the inadequacy of the information he has gathered, he confesses openly in chapter XI: "I did not find out anymore about this, and what I have written down is of little help." As if these difficulties were not enough, one must also consider that Spanish was not Pané's native language. In commenting on his extracts from Pané's testimony, Las Casas remarks: "All this Fray Ramón says he has understood from the Indians. He says some other things that are confused and of little substance, as a simple person who did not speak our Castilian tongue altogether well, since he was a Catalan by birth."[23]

These, then, are the myriad difficulties that beset the text I have retranslated and edited. With the original manuscript lost, Ulloa's version becomes the surviving text most closely linked to the text Pané wrote, and thus I follow the first edition of that translation with the greatest possible fidelity. For the sake of that fidelity, I abstain from any stylistic

23. Las Casas, *Apologética historia*, chapter 167; in the cited edition, p. 447.

retouching, either to avoid the repetition of words and syntactic turns of phrase, to suppress redundancies, or to improve the prose by the addition of qualities that Pané's modest pen lacked. If the reader finds the style monotonous and even at times pedestrian, such is the style of Ulloa's version and thus, very likely, would also have been that of the "humble friar." What is of interest here is faithfulness to the text and not literary embellishments.

With regard to Taíno words, if it were a matter of simply making a paleographic transcription of a manuscript, the proper procedure would be, of course, to reproduce them exactly as they appear in the text. Because there is no original manuscript, I must resort to another solution. As we have seen, Ulloa attempted to adapt to Italian spellings the words that Pané had transcribed in accordance with Spanish orthographic practices, but Ulloa did not observe strict rules, and he committed frequent variations and omissions. A comparison of his transcriptions with those of Anghiera and Las Casas makes apparent that he often confused *u* and *n, e* and *o, c* and *r,* and that he represented with the Italian spelling *gi* both the sounds that in modern Spanish are differentiated as *j* and *y.* In such circumstances, I have had to choose between reproducing the terms as Ulloa wrote them, with the knowledge that they are corrupted, or attempting an improved reading by re-Hispanicizing those words and at times reconstructing their spelling. In spite of the obvious risk, I have opted for the second solution. The exact spellings that appear in Ulloa and the variants found in Anghiera, Las Casas, and other sources are given in the notes. I also indicate in the notes the reasons—or doubts—that prompted me to choose the form I have given in the text, and I suggest, whenever possible, the meaning the word could have had in the Taíno language. In this way, those who may wish to read the *Account* without interruption will not have to deal with doubtful sixteenth-century Italian forms improperly interpolated in a twentieth-century Spanish translation or with outworn variants of indigenous terms that today are fully incorporated into our language. Those who may wish to examine the reconstruction question, both in its textual aspect and in its ethnolinguistic dimension, will find in the notes the data I have been able to contribute on the subject. They should be aware, however, that some of the suggested spellings are inevitably of a hypothetical nature. When one works with a language that became extinct nearly five centuries ago and of which only tenuous vestiges have survived, the work of reconstruction and clarification cannot always produce certainties. The reader may take this effort, thus, as an attempt to define problems whose solutions we are scarcely beginning to envision.

The principal goal of this edition is to serve as a basis for future anthropological, mythological, and linguistic inquiries. I have thought it useful, therefore, to include as appendixes the versions written by those who handled the manuscript directly—that is, the brief information given by Columbus, Anghiera's summary, and the extracts transcribed by Las Casas. Scholars may more easily consult the passages that interest them and see in their proper context the quotations referred to in the notes. In order to maintain the linguistic unity of the edition, Columbus's paragraphs and Anghiera's summary are also included in new English translations based on new Spanish translations.

Finally, it may well be that Pané's manuscript, sought for in vain,[24] might reappear one day. Likewise, when more precise methods have been developed for the study of particular Amerindian languages and myths, perhaps some of the doubts will be resolved that today have only been sketched out. The important thing, in any case, is that this translation might allow other scholars to base their inquiries on a less corrupted text.[25]

24. I have learned that UNESCO is contemplating the project of cataloging all the Spanish archives. If such a project were to be carried out, perhaps the manuscript will be found, if indeed it is still in Spain.

25. Basing my work on this text and amplifying the scope of the notes, I have published the article "El mundo mítico de los Taínos: Notas sobre el Ser Supremo," *Thesaurus, Boletín del Instituto Caro y Cuervo* 22 (1967): 378–93, reprinted in the *Revista Dominicana de Arqueología y Antropología* 1, no. 1 (January–June 1971): 181–200. This article has been incorporated into the book *Mitología y artes prehispánicas de las Antillas* (Mexico City, 1975). I take up the topic once again, in order to emphasize its relevance in the plastic arts and letters of the Antilles, in "Fray Ramón Pané o el rescate de un mundo mítico," *La Revista del Centro de Estudios Avanzados de Puerto Rico y el Caribe,* no. 3 (July–December 1986): 2–8, and more recently in "Fray Ramón Pané, descubridor del hombre americano," *Revista de Estudios Hispánicos* (1992): 35–46; "Las dos caras de la conquista: De las opuestas imágenes del otro al debate sobre la dignidad del indio," in *De palabra y otra en el Nuevo Mundo,* vol. 1 *Imágenes interétnicas,* edited by Miguel León Portilla et al. (Madrid, 1992), pp. 63–85; and "Tiempo y espacio en el pensamiento cosmológico taíno," *La Torre, Nueva Época* 8, no. 29 (January–March 1994): 5–23. See also Irving Rouse and José Juan Arrom, "The Taínos: Principal Inhabitants of Columbus' Indies," in *Circa 1492: Art in the Age of Exploration,* edited by Jay A. Levenson (New Haven and London, 1991), pp. 509–13. Also, for a very complete and valuable study of the Taínos, see Irving Rouse, *The Taínos: Rise and Fall of the People Who Greeted Columbus* (New Haven and London, 1992).

AN ACCOUNT
OF THE
ANTIQUITIES
OF THE INDIANS

An Account of the Antiquities of the Indians, Diligently Gathered by Fray Ramón,[1] a Man Who Knows Their Language, by Order[1a] of the Admiral

I, Fray Ramón, a humble friar of the Order of Saint Jerome, am writing what I have been able to discover and understand of the beliefs and idolatries of the Indians, and of how they worship their gods, by order of the illustrious Lord Admiral and Viceroy and Governor of the Islands and Mainland of the Indies. I will now consider these matters in this present account.

In worshiping the idols they keep at home, which they call zemis,[2] each one observes a particular manner and superstition. They believe that he is in heaven and is immortal, and that no one can see him, and that he has a mother. But He has no beginning,[3] and they call him Yú-

1. Ulloa: *fra Roman*. For the reasons explained in the introductory study, *Roman* will be changed to *Ramón* throughout the translation.

1a. I use *mandado* and not *mandato* (mandate or order) in order to coincide with the sixteenth-century spelling. Oviedo, for example, writes: "Por cuyo mandado hizo este descubrimiento" or "By whose order he made this discovery" (*Historia general y natural de las Indias* [Seville, 1535], book 2, chap. 4).

2. Ulloa: *cemini*, an Italianate plural of *cemi*. Subsequent notes show that Ulloa vacillates among the singular forms, *cemi, cimi, cimiche*, and the plural, *cemini, cimini*. Anghiera, latinizing the spelling, writes *zeme, zemes*. Las Casas, more familiar with the Taíno language, explains: "They had some idols or good luck statues, and these were generally called *çemí*, the final syllable long and stressed." Las Casas's Hispanicization is what has become dominant in modern Spanish: singular, *cemí*; plural, *cemíes*. (Because the forms *zemi*, singular, and *zemis*, plural—based on Anghiera's Latinate spelling—have come into accepted usage in English, they will be written thus in this translation, although *cemi* and *cemies* would be more correct.)

3. Ulloa's translation is confused: "Tengono che sia come in cielo immortale, e che alcun non possa vederlo, & che ha madre, & ch'ei non habbia principio." Las Casas paraphra-

cahu Bagua Maórocoti,[4] and they call his mother Atabey, Yermao, Guacar, Apito, and Zuimaco, which are five names.[5] Those about whom I
am writing are from the Island of Hispaniola because I know nothing
whatsoever of the other islands, for I have never seen them.[6] They know
likewise from whence they came, and where the sun and the moon had
their beginning, and how the sea was made, and where the dead go. And

ses Pané's text as follows: "The people of this island Hispaniola had a certain faith in and
knowledge of a one and true God, who was immortal and invisible, for none could see
him, who had no beginning, whose dwelling place and residence is heaven."

4. Ulloa: *Iocahuuague Maorocon;* Anghiera: *Iocauna Guamaonocon;* Las Casas: *Yocahu Vagua
Maorocoti.* The form recorded by Las Casas has been selected, with the spelling and accentuation duly modernized, because it was the only one of the three carried over directly
into Spanish. These terms probably mean "giver of cassava," "master of the sea," "con-
ceived without male intervention."

One should remember that in the era in which Pané was writing, the *h* represented an
aspirated sound similar to that of the English *h* or the modern Spanish *j*. Thus, words that
were written *higüera, hobo,* or *hutia* today are pronounced *jigüera, jobo, jutia*. As a result,
in this and other instances when an *h* appears before a vowel, it should be pronounced like
the Spanish *j*: *Yúcaju, Guajayona, Itiba Cajubaba, Mároju,* etc.

5. Ulloa: "Atabei, Iermaoguacar, Apito & Zuimaco, che son cinque nomi." One should
note that written in this fashion they are only four. Anghiera gives five, but some are
totally different: *Attabeira, Mamona, Guacarapita, Iella, Guimazoa.* Las Casas is of little
help on this occasion, for he says only: "God had a mother, whose name was Atabex, and
his brother Guaca, and other relatives in like fashion." Of these names, it is possible that
Attabeira (from *atté*, the vocative of "mother" and the attached suffix *beira* "water") is the
equivalent of Mother of the Waters; *Guacar* could have been *Wa-katti ~ Wa-kairi* (from
wa- "our" and *katti ~ kairi* "moon," a word also related to "tide" and "menstruation").

Mamona, which appears in Anghiera's text but not in the others, could have been a mistaken reading of *Mamano*, perhaps by analogy with *mamona* or *mamola*. Brasseur de Bour-
bourg, in a little-known vocabulary of the Indo Antillean languages, writes: "MAMANO,
s. titre de la divinité" (*Quelques vestiges d'un vocabulaire de l'ancienne langue de Haití et ses
dialectes,* published as an appendix to his translation of *Relations des choses de Yucatan de
Diego de Landa* [Paris, 1864]). If it were *Mamano*, it can be analyzed as *mama* "mother"
and *-no,* sign of the feminine plural, and it would be equivalent to "mother-s" or perhaps
more likely to "Universal Mother." (See Nancy P. Hickerson, "Ethnolinguistic Notes from
Lexicons of Lokono [Arawak]," *International Journal of American Linguistics* 19 [1953], 183.)

A free translation of the above epithets, more attentive to their sacred character than
to their literal meaning, would read thus: Mother of the Waters; Lady of the Moon, the
Tides, and Maternity; Universal Mother.

6. Las Casas broadens the geographic framework of Pané's observations when he comments: "One should know that the peoples of this Hispaniola and the Island of Cuba and
that which we call San Juan and that of Jamaica and the islands of the Bahamas, and generally all the rest that are almost in a row . . . from close to the Mainland called Florida,
up to the tip of the peninsula of Paria . . . and also along the sea coast, the peoples of the
Mainland along that shore of the Gulf of Paria . . . almost all those people had one kind
of religion."

they believe the dead appear to them along the road when they travel alone because they do not appear when many of them travel together. Their ancestors have made them believe all this, for they do not know how to read, nor can they count except up to ten.[7]

CHAPTER I

Concerning the place from which the Indians
have come and in what manner

There is a province in Hispaniola called Caonao[8] in which there is a mountain called Cauta,[9] which has two caves. The name of one of these is Cacibajagua,[10] and Amayaúna[11] the other. The majority of the people

---

7. The Taínos, like other Amerindian peoples — and in part the French — counted by a vigesimal system. For *five* they said "hand," for *ten* "two hands," for *twenty* "man," for *eighty* "four men." See, among others, Raymond Breton, *Dictionnaire caraïbe-français*, reprinted by Jules Platzmann (Leipzig, 1892), p. 78; Daniel G. Brinton, "The Arawak Language of Guiana in Its Linguistic and Ethnological Relations," in *Transactions of the American Philosophical Society*, New Series 14 (1871), 430 and 431; Carl F. von Martius, *Beiträge zur Ethnographie und Sprachenkunde Amerikas zumal Brasiliens.* II. *Zur Sprachenkunde* (Leipzig, 1867), p. 310; and José Gumilla, *El Orinoco ilustrado* (Madrid, 1741), p. 506.

8. Ulloa: *Caanau;* Anghiera: *Caunana.* Other chroniclers write *Caunao* or *Caonao.* Both forms survive as names of places and bodies of water in the Antilles. It means "place where there is gold."

9. Ulloa: *canta;* Anghiera: *Cauta.* One should note that Ulloa frequently misreads the *u;* as we have just seen above in note 8, he confused it with an *a;* here he mistakes it for an *n.* In support of Pietro Martire's reading one could add that the largest river in Cuba is called the *Cauto,* likely a Taíno word. Further, the word *kauta* is used in the Arawak language to designate a tree whose ashes, mixed with clay, are used in the making of pottery. See J. Crevaux, P. Sagot, and L. Adam, *Grammaire et vocabulaires roucouyenne, arrouague, piapoco et d'autres langues de la région des Guyanes* (Paris, 1882), p. 134.

One should keep in mind that Cauta does not refer to just any geographic irregularity; it corresponds to the sacred mount or magic mountain of several mythologies in both the Old and the New Worlds — Mount Olympus, for example.

10. Ulloa: *Cacibagiagua;* Anghiera: *Cazibaxagua;* thus, we have chosen to write *Cacibajagua.* *Caciba* seems to be the same word that written *casimba* or *cacimba* — with an epenthetic *m* generated by the nasalization of the vowel before a nasal consonant — continues to be used from the Antilles to the Platte River to designate a hollow place in a terrain. *Jagua* is the name of a tree common in the Antilles (*Genipa americana*), and it survives as a toponym in several places. *Cacibajagua* would be the equivalent, thus, of Cacimba or Jagua Cave. (See also chapter XXV, note 126.)

11. Ulloa: *Amaiauua;* Anghiera: *Amaiauna.* Once again, Pietro Martire's reading is the choice. *Iauna, iouna* has in Arawak the sense of "price, value, compensation." *Ama-* could be the privative *ma-*, "without, lacking." *Amayaúna* would be, thus, the name of the cave from whence emerged those without merit, value, or importance — that is to say, the non-Taínos.

who populated the island came from Cacibajagua.[12] When they were living in those caves, these people stood watch at night, and they had entrusted this task to a man by the name of Mácocael.[13] Because one day he was late in returning to the door, they say, the Sun carried him off. Because the Sun had carried away this man for his lack of vigilance, they closed the door against him. Thus it was that he was turned into stone near the door. Afterwards, they say, others who had gone to fish were captured by the Sun, and they were changed into trees they call *jobos* [hog plum trees],[14] and they are also called *mirabálanos* [myrobalans]. The reason why Mácocael was keeping watch and standing guard was in order to see where he would send or distribute the people, and it seems that he tarried to his great misfortune.

CHAPTER II
How the men were separated from the women
It happened that a man whose name was Guahayona[15] told another who was called Yahubaba[16] to go and gather a plant called *digo*,[17] with which they clean their bodies when they go to bathe. He went out before dawn, and the Sun caught him along the road, and he was turned into a bird

12. The Taínos belonged to the Arawak family and in fact reached the Antilles from the northern zone of South America. Furthermore, many peoples of the world have myths that posit an autocthonous or earthly origin for man as opposed to his bisexual or biological origin.

13. Ulloa: *Marocael;* Anghiera: *Machochael.* If Ulloa read the toponym *Macorís* as *Maroris,* it is plausible that here as well he may have confused the *c* and the *r* and read *Marocael* in place of *Macocael.* We select, thus, the reading of Pietro Martire, Hispanicizing once again the spelling. The word seems to be related to *ákoke* "eyelid," and thus Mácocael would be "He of the lidless eyes."

14. Ulloa: *iobi,* that is to say "*jobos.*" The *jobo* (*Spondias lutea*) is a very common tree in tropical America; it bears a yellow fruit similar to the plum. Thus, Pané, and Anghiera following Pané, believed it was myrobalan.

15. Here and in three other instances in this and the two following chapters the text reads: *Guagugiona.* Pietro Martire, following this first spelling, writes *Vagoniona.* But beginning in chapter V (note 28), the word appears eleven times as *Guahagiona.* Could it be that Pané, hearing more clearly, corrected the spelling as he wrote? Based on that possibility and to avoid confusion, we have modernized the word in every instance to *Guahayona.* See also note 38.

16. Ulloa: *Giadruuaua.* The cluster *dr* may be a reading in error for *h.* It reappears as an *h* a few lines below in the mention of the bird whose name is based on this character (note 18). And it reappears as an *h* in *Cahuba[ba]yael* (chapter VIII, note 50), and in *Itiba Tahubaba* or *Cahubaba* (chapter IX, note 56). Perhaps *Yahubaba, Tahubaba,* and *Cahubaba* are variants of the same word.

17. It appears thus in the text. The identification of this plant creates a confusing problem that is alluded to below in Pané's text. See note 19.

that sings in the morning, like the nightingale, and is called *yahuba-bayael.*[18] Seeing that the man whom he had sent to gather the *digo* did not return, Guahayona resolved to leave the said Cacibajagua cave.

CHAPTER III
How the indignant Guahayona resolved to leave, seeing
that those men whom he had sent to gather the digo *for*
bathing did not return
And he said to the women: "Leave your husbands and let us go to other lands and let us take much *güeyo.*[19] Leave your children, and let us take only the plant with us, for afterwards we will return for them."

CHAPTER IV
Guahayona departed with all the women and went in search of other lands, and he arrived in Matininó,[20] where he immediately left the women and went to another region, called Guanín;[21] and they had left the small children next to a stream. Later, they say, when hunger began to trouble them, they wept and called to their mothers who had gone away; and the parents could not succor the children, who were crying out from hunger to their mothers, saying "mama" in order to cry, but truly in order to ask for the teat. And crying thus and asking for the teat, saying "toa, toa"[22] like one who asks for something with great desire

18. Ulloa: *Giahuba Bagiael.* The two words, joined, seem to correspond to the same *Cahu-baba[ya]el* of chapter VIII, note 50.
19. The text reads *gioie,* which in Italian means "jewels." Chapters XVI (note 95) and XVII (note 100) indicate that *gioie* is an erroneous reading of the name of the plant called *güeyo* in chapter XVII. One should note further that the following sentence reiterates that they carry "only the plant." Were the *güeyo* and the *digo* the same plant or two different ones? As for what the *güeyo* may have been, see note 100, and for the *digo,* note 130.
20. Ulloa: *Matinino;* Anghiera: *Mathininó.* As for the accentuation, Anghiera declares (*Década* 3, book 7, chap. 1): "The island of Matininó . . . accented on the last syllable." According to Morison, this island is Martinique. However, according to Father Breton, the indigenous name of Martinique was not Matininó but *Ioüanacaera*—that is to say, *Igua-nacairi,* "Island of Iguanas" (*Dictionnaire,* p. 412). I am inclined to think that Matininó is a mythical landscape and not a geographical location.
21. Thus in the text. Andrés Bernáldez, friend and confidante of Columbus, wrote: "The *cacique* wore around his neck a metal jewel from an island in that region called *Guaní,* which is very fine" (*Memorias del reinado de los Reyes Católicos que escribía el bachiller Andrés Bernáldez, Cura de los Palacios* [Madrid, 1962], p. 331). See notes 39, 41, and 43.
22. Ulloa: *too, too.* Anghiera: *toa, toa. Toa* survives as the name of several rivers in Cuba, the most important of which is near Baracoa. It is possible that *toa* in fact meant "water." See note 25.

and very softly,[23] they were transformed into little animals, like frogs,[24] which are called *tona*,[25] because of the way they were asking for the teat. And in this way all those men were left without women.

CHAPTER V
How afterwards there were once again women on the said Island of Hispaniola, which before was called Haití,[26] and the inhabitants call it by this name; and they called it and the other islands Bohío[27]

And because they have neither writing nor letters, they cannot give a good account of how they have heard this from their ancestors, and therefore they do not all say the same thing, nor can one even write down in an orderly fashion what they tell. When Guahayona[28] left, the one who carried away all the women, he took the wives of his *cacique* [chief or chieftain][29] as well, who was called Anacacuya,[30] deceiving him

---

23. The text reads *molto adagio*, *"muy despacio."* Bourne translates this phrase as "very urgently" (*Columbus*, 13). Other translators interpret it in an equally imaginative fashion. They forget that *despacio* is the equivalent of "in a soft voice." Joan Corominas documents this use in several American countries as well as in Asturias and other regions of Spain in his "Indianorrománica: Occidentalismos americanos," *Revista de Filología Hispánica* 6 (1944), 231.

24. The text: *nane* "dwarves," an error for *rane* "frogs." Anghiera leaves no doubt as to the reading: "in rane conversi."

25. Ulloa: *tona*. The words *tona*, *toona*, and *tuna* mean "water" in Carib, Taruma, Trío, Rucuyén, Carijona, and other Amerindian languages.

26. Ulloa: *Aiti*. Anghiera elsewhere (*Década* 3, book 7, chap. 1) explains: "The names the first inhabitants gave to Hispaniola were, first, *Quizquella*, later, *Haití* . . . But Haití means ruggedness in their ancient language, and thus they named the entire island . . . for the harsh appearance of its mountains." Regarding the meaning of *Haití*, Pedro Henríquez Ureña points out: "Name of the highest peak in the ancient mountainous region of Cibao, according to Las Casas (*Apologética historia*, Chapters 6 and 197), from which 'this whole island was designated and named'; the peasants still call the mountains *haitíses*" (*El español en Santo Domingo* [Buenos Aires, 1940], p. 209).

27. Ulloa: *Bouhi*. Although there are numerous variants of this term (see note 85), *bohío* is the form accepted today to designate a type of rustic hut, with bark or wood walls and a thatched palm roof. Originally it meant "house or habitation," and thus Pané gathered that Hispaniola "and the other islands are called Bohío," an obvious synecdoche for islands that are our "house or habitation," our ancestral home.

28. Ulloa: *Guahagiona*. One should remember that in the three previous chapters the name appears written as *Guagugiona* and that here it is written *Guahagiona*. See also note 38.

29. Accepting the Taíno world, Ulloa transcribes it thus: *cacique*. The Spanish translated it as "king, governor, administrator." In Taíno, it was perhaps *ka-siqua* "with-house"—that is to say, head of the house or the houses.

30. Ulloa: *Anacacuia*. *Annaka* in Arawak is "center, middle"; *cuiya* could be either *kuya*

---

like he deceived the others. And also a brother-in-law of Guahayona's, called Anacacuya, who was traveling with him, went into the sea, and the said Guahayona, who was in the canoe,[31] said to his brother-in-law: "Look what a handsome *cobo*[32] there is in the water." This *cobo* is the sea snail. And when he was looking at the water to see the *cobo*, his brother-in-law Guahayona took him by the feet and threw him into the sea. And so he took all the women for himself, and he left them in Matininó,[33] where they say today there are nothing but women. And he went to another island, which is called Guanín, and it was so named because of what he carried away from it when he went there.

CHAPTER VI
How Guahayona returned to the said Cauta,[34] *from where he had taken the women*
They say that when Guahayona was in the land to which he had gone, he saw that he had left a woman in the sea, which gave him great pleasure, and at once he sought many lavations to bathe himself because he was

---

"spirit" (as in the syntagma *konoko-kuya* recorded as "bush-spirit") or *kuyuha ~ koeia* "star, constellation." That is to say, "Central Spirit" or perhaps "Star of the Center."

This linguistic analysis has been confirmed by Sebastián Robiou Lamarche, who postulates, based on rigorous astronomical research, that Anacacuya is the mythic representation of the Pole Star and that the passage codifies Taíno meteorological knowledge of phenomena related to the seasons of rain and drought. See his revealing study, "Astronomy in Taino Mythology," *Archaeoastronomy* 7 (1984): 110–15. He has continued this research in "Ida y vuelta a Guanín: Un ensayo sobre la cosmovisión taína," *Latin America Studies* 34 (1986): 459–98).

31. Ulloa transcribes this Taíno word just as it appears here: *canoa*. On the possible origin of the word, see Douglas Taylor, "Spanish *Canoa* and Its Congeners," *International Journal of American Linguistics* 23, no. 3 (July 1957): 242–44.

32. *Cobo.* Thus in the text. Anghiera comments in *Década* 7, book 1, chapter 2: "Under the water they find a certain kind of jewel they greatly esteem, of red conch shells, which they wear hanging from the ears. But they take another more precious kind from the great spiral conch. . . . That conch they call *cohobo*, and its little stone *cohibici*." Because "stone" is *ciba*, one may suppose that Anghiera transposed the *b* and the *c* in what should read *cohibici*. Ulloa writes *colecibi* (see note 40).

33. The text reads "lasciò quelle di Matanino"—that is to say, "he left those from Matininó." Because Guahayona went to the other island without taking any of those women, I infer that the reading should have been "he left them in Matininó." This correction is in accord with the narration as it continues in chapter VI. I also correct *Matanino* to *Matininó*. The legend that there were only women on Matininó gave rise to the Spanish imaginings of Amazons everywhere. The legend is related to the name of the island, which can be analyzed as *Ma-iti-ni-no*, "without-father-s."

34. Ulloa: *Canta.* This is corrected to *Cauta*, as in chapter 1, note 9.

full of those sores we call the French disease.[35] She placed him then in a *guanara*, which means a separate place;[36] and thus while he was there, he recovered from his sores. Afterwards he asked her leave to continue his journey, and she gave it to him. This woman was called Guabonito.[37] And Guahayona changed his name, calling himself henceforth Albeborael Guahayona.[38] And the woman Guabonito gave Albeborael Guahayona many *guanines* and many *cibas*[39] so that he would wear them tied to his arms, for in those lands the *cibas*[40] are made of stones very much like marble, and they wear them tied to their arms and around their necks, and they wear the *guanines* in their ears, in which they make holes when they are little, and they are made of a metal almost like a florin.[41] It is said that Guabonito, Albeborael[42] Guahayona, and Albeborael's father

35. The French disease. It is also called *bubas* or *syphilis*, which evidently existed in America before 1492. On the debated question of the American or European origin of that disease, see Samuel E. Morison, *Admiral of the Ocean Sea*, 2 vols. (Boston, 1942), 2:193–218. Based on paleopathological examinations of Taíno bone remains, Dr. Fernando Luna Calderón has established that indeed "the disease was present in the Greater Antilles before the discovery of America." See "Paleopatología de los grupos taínos de la Hispaniola," in Seminario sobre la situación de la investigación de la cultura taína, *La cultura taína* (Las culturas de América en la época del descubrimiento) (Madrid, 1983), pp. 174–75.
36. *Guanara* has survived in parts of Cuba as the name of a dove that lives in remote mountain areas (Esteban Rodríguez Herrera, *Léxico mayor de Cuba*, vol. 2 [Havana, 1959]). In Guajiro, another language in the Arawak family, *guanöru* is "disease" (Rafael Celedón, *Gramática, catecismo i vocabulario de la lengua goajira* [Paris, 1878], p. 96).
37. The text has here *Guabonito*, but a few lines below *Gualonito*.
38. Ulloa: *Biberoci Guahagiona*, but a few lines below he calls him *Albeborael Guahagiona* (note 42). The discrepancy in first names could be due to the fact that in *Biberoci* he read a *c*, where it was likely an *e: Biberoei*. This would correspond to an ending, frequent among proper names, that appears as *-ey*, *-ex*, or *-el (Guarioney ~ Guarionex ~ Guarionel)*. Considering both terms, it would turn out that *[Al]biberoei* and *Albeborael* are, in fact, variants of the same name, and therefore I give in every case the more complete of the two. (On another probable confusion between *c* and *e*, see note 149.)
   With regard to the second name, the spelling change from *Guagugiona* to *Guahagiona* could be explained by the fact that *wahajia ~ wahaddia* is in Arawak equivalent to "later, henceforward." It is a very widespread custom among Arawak peoples to change one's name after recovering from a serious illness. See Walter E. Roth, *An Inquiry into the Animism and Folk-lore of the Guiana Indians* (Washington, D.C., 1915), p. 345.
39. Ulloa: *guanini . . . cibe*. Las Casas and other Spanish chroniclers write *guanines* and *cibas*.
40. Ulloa: *colecibi*. These would be the *cibas*, made from the conch of the *cobo* (*Strombus gigas*), which Pietro Martire called *cohibici*. See note 32.
41. Guanín is an alloy of gold, silver, and copper. See Paul Rivet, "L'orfèvrerie précolombienne des Antilles, des Guyanes et du Vénézuela, dans ses rapports avec l'orfèvrerie et la métallurgie des autres régions américaines," *Journal de la Société des Américanistes de Paris*, Nouvelle série 15 (1923): 183–213.
42. Ulloa: *Albeborael Guahagiona*. Cf. note 38. Mercedes López-Baralt has written a bril-

were the origin of these *guanines*. Guahayona stayed in the land with his father, who was called Hiauna.[43] His father called him Híaguali Guanín, which means son of Hiauna, and henceforth he was called Guanín, and this is his name today. And because they have neither letters nor writing, they do not know how to tell such fables well, nor can I write them well.[44] Therefore, I believe that I put first what ought to be last and the last first. But everything I write, they tell it thus, in the manner I am writing it, and thus I set it down as I have understood it from the people of the country.

CHAPTER VII

How there were once again women on the aforementioned Island of Haiti,[45] which is now called Hispaniola

They say that one day the men went to bathe, and while they were in the water, it rained a great deal, and they felt a great desire to have women; and that often when it rained, they went to search for the tracks of their

---

liant exegesis of these episodes, applying analytical methods based on the universal structure of myths. Her research reveals that Guahayona, a Taíno cultural hero, is the protagonist of the origin myth, the rites of passage, the sexual initiation, the acquisition of power, and the chieftain's investiture. See her book *El mito taíno: Lévi-Strauss en las Antillas* (Río Piedras, 1985), pp. 144-56.

43. Ulloa: *Hia Guaili Guanin . . . Hiauna.* This reading is very confused. If *Hia Guaili* "means son of Hiauna," the transcription should have been *Hiaunael* because the suffix *-el*, according to Pané's own reports (chapter IX), means "son of." But it could also have been that the syllables were incorrectly separated: joined, they would read *Híaguaili*, a transcription very similar to *Híali*, which is the form recorded by Breton. See note 44. On the other hand, in some regions of Cuba and the Dominican Republic, the hummingbird is called *guaní*, an indigenous word.

44. The extreme confusion of the entire paragraph could be due to the fact that Pané did not understand very well what they told him. Happily, I have come across analogous versions of the same myth among the island Caribs (Breton, *Dictionnaire*, p. 293), the Arawaks and Guaraos (Roth, *An Inquiry*, p. 256), the indigenous people of the Jamundá River (Paul Ehrenreich, *Die Mythen und Legenden der Südamerikanischen Urvölker* [Berlin, 1905], p. 37), the Waiwai (Niels Fock, *Waiwai: Religion and Society of an Amazonian Tribe* [Copenhagen, 1963], pp. 54-56), and even in a tribe of Eskimos (Knud Rasmussen, *The Netsilik Eskimos: Social Life and Spiritual Culture. Report of the Fifth Thule Expedition*, vol. 8, 1-2 [Copenhagen, 1931], pp. 235-36). According to these versions, *Híali* is the son of the incestuous relations of a man with his own sister, and caught in the act, he fled the tribe and was transformed into the moon. Douglas Taylor, who has also collected the tale among the Caribs in Dominica, reports that *Híali* means "He-who-has-become-brilliant" ("Tales and Legends of the Dominica Caribs," *Journal of American Folklore* 65 [1952], 269). See also my article, "Tiempo y espacio en el pensamiento cosmológico taíno," mentioned in note 25 of the introductory study.

45. Ulloa: *Aiti.*

women, but they could not find any sign of them. But that day, as they were bathing, they say that they saw some kind of persons fall from some trees, coming down among the branches. These forms were neither men nor women, nor did they have the sex of male or female, and they went to seize them, but they fled as if they were eels.[46] Therefore, by order of their *cacique,* because they could not seize them, they called two or three men to see how many there were and to seek out for each one a man who was *caracaracol*[47] because their hands were rough, and thus they might hold on to them tightly. They told the *cacique* there were four of them,[48] and so they took four men who were *caracaracoles.* The said *caracaracol* is a disease like mange that makes the body very rough. After they had seized them, they took counsel on what they could do to make them women because they did not have the sex of male or female.

CHAPTER VIII

How they found a solution so that they would be women
They looked for a bird called *inriri,*[49] formerly called *inriri cahubaba-yael,*[50] which makes holes in the trees and in our language is called a woodpecker. And likewise they took those women without the sex of male or female, and they tied their hands and feet, and they brought the aforementioned bird and tied it to their bodies. And believing they were trees, the bird began his customary work, picking and burrowing holes in the place where the sex of women is generally located. And in this way the Indians say that they had women, according to the stories of the most elderly. Because I wrote it down in haste and did not have sufficient paper, I was not able to write down in that place what I had copied down elsewhere by mistake; but in any case, I have not been in error because they believe everything just as I have written it down. Let us return now to what I ought to have written first, that is, to the opinion they have about the origin and beginning of the sea.

46. The text: *aquile,* "eagles," error for *anguille,* "eels." Anghiera confirms this reading: "Veluti anguillae de manibus eorum labuntur": "like eels they slipped from their hands."
47. Thus in the text. Pané explains the meaning immediately, in the same sentence.
48. It is no accident that these asexual beings were four in number. Four is the sacred number of the Amerindian cosmogonies. And the brothers or sisters created by the gods are generally four in number. See note 57.
49. Here in the text: *inriri,* but below, *inrire.*
50. Ulloa: *inrire cahuuaial.* The second word was perhaps *Cahuua[ua]ia[e]l,* "son or descendent of Cahubaba" (see notes 16, 18, and 56).

CHAPTER IX

How they say the sea was made

There was a man called Yaya, whose name they do not know;[51] and his son was called Yayael, which means son of Yaya.[52] Because Yayael wanted to kill his father, the latter sent him into exile, and thus he was exiled for four months;[52a] and afterwards his father killed him and put his bones in a gourd[53] and hung it from the roof of his house, where it was hanging for some time.[54] It happened one day that Yaya, desiring to see his son, said to his wife: "I want to see our son Yayael." And she was glad, and taking down the gourd, she turned it over to see the bones of their son. And many fish, large and small, emerged from it. Whereby, seeing that those bones had been changed into fish, they resolved to eat them.

They say, thus, that one day when Yaya had gone to see his *conucos*,[55] which means possessions, which were his inheritance, four men arrived who were the sons of one woman, who was called Itiba Cahubaba,[56] all

51. Ulloa: *Giaia.* The apparent contradiction of their not knowing his name immediately after it has been declared that his name was *Yaya* is explained if one takes into account that in Arawak *Ia* means "spirit, essence, primary cause of life" (C. H. de Goeje, *The Arawak Language of Guiana* [Amsterdam, 1928], pp. 45, 142, and 204). Having the form of a superlative by duplication, *Yaya* is the equivalent of "Supreme Spirit."

52. This is a joined suffix, *-el*, whose meaning Pané clarifies below. On other occasions *-el* also appears written as *-ex: Guarionel* or *Guarionex* (see note 125).

52a. These four months do not correspond to our chronometrical concepts; they represent an indeterminate mythic time related once again to the four brothers and the four quadrants of the universe.

53. The text: *zucca* "gourd." In fact, it would have been a *güira (Crescentia cujete)*, the bark of which, used as a vessel, is still called *higüera* or *jigüera* in the Antilles, a Taíno name.

54. The custom of hanging the bones in a basket *(jaba)* or keeping them in a funerary urn was noted by Columbus on his first voyage (*Diario,* Thursday, November 29), and Pané confirms it in chapter XV.

55. Ulloa: *conichi,* an Italianization of the Spanish form *conucos.* In Arawak, *kunuku* is "wood, forest."

56. Ulloa: *Itiba, Tahuuaua.* The word *Itiba* perhaps contains the root recorded in Arawak as *ite ~ üttü ~ üthe* "blood." If there is any relation between Taíno and Tupí, the word would be related to the adjective *tuíuara* "bloody, bloodied" (Conde Ermano Stradelli, *Vocabularios da lingua geral portuguez-nheêngatú e nheêngatú-portuguez* [Rio de Janeiro, 1929], p. 682). Regarding *Tahubaba,* based on the fact that the *t* is often interchanged with *k* in the Arawak languages, it could also have been *Cahubaba* (see note 16). In this matter, it is worth pointing out that several places in Cuba have the name of *Cajobabo* (Julián Vivanco, *El lenguaje de los Indios de Cuba* [Havana, 1946], p. 47). Furthermore, on the western bank of the Mamoré River, a tributary of the Amazon, lives a tribe called *Kayubaba* (G. de Créqui-Monfort and P. Rivet, "La langue Kayuvaya," *International Journal of American Linguistics* 1 [1917–1918]: 245–63, and Harold Key, "Phonotactics of Kuyavava," *International Journal of American Linguistics* 27 [1961]: 143–50). In the event that such a

from one womb and identical. When that woman died in childbirth, they opened her up and took out the four said sons,[57] and the first they took out was *caracaracol,* which means mangy,[58] and that *caracaracol* was called [Deminán];[59] the others did not have names.

CHAPTER X

How the four identical sons of Itiba Cahubaba, who died in childbirth, went together to take Yaya's gourd, which held his son Yayael,[60] who had been transformed into fishes, and none dared to seize it except Deminán[61] Caracaracol, who took it down, and everyone ate their fill of fish

And while they were eating, they heard Yaya coming back from his possessions, and in that fix wanting to hang up the gourd urgently, they did not hang it well so that it fell to the earth and broke. They say that so much water came out of that gourd that it filled up the whole earth, and many fish came out with the water; and thus it was, they say, that the sea had its origin. Afterwards they left that place, and they found a man called Conel,[62] who was mute.

---

relationship did exist with Tupí-Guaraní, *kayu* in Tupí is "old, weighed down with years" (P. C. Tatevin, *La langue tapïhïya dite tupí ou neêngatu* [Vienna, 1910], p. 102). In such a case, this Bloodied Old Mother would correspond, within the American mythologies, to *Pachamama,* the Mother Earth of the Incas, and to *Coatlicue,* the Mother Earth, the Great Birth Mother of the Aztecs.

57. In this myth, the Four Twins seem to represent the four cardinal points. This interpretation agrees with the following commentary by Daniel G. Brinton: "The number four, sacred in all American religions, and the key to their symbolism, [is] derived from the cardinal points. . . . The cardinal points identified with the Four Winds, who in the myths are the four ancestors of the human race" (*The Myths of the New World* [New York, 1876], p. 68). They would be the equivalent of the four Tezcatlipocas of the Aztec cosmogony and the four Bacabs of the Maya. See also note 48.

58. Douglas Taylor suggests that the Taíno word *caracaracol* is perhaps the same as the island Carib *kara karacoti,* in which the attributive prefix *ka-* is first attached to *ura* "skin" and then to *uraku* "mange." "A Note on the Arawakan Affiliation of Taino," *International Journal of American Linguistics* 20 (1954), 153.

59. A lacuna marked in the text by an ellipsis. Thereafter it will be seen that the name missing here should be *Deminán.* Cf. notes 61 and 67.

60. These names appear as has been indicated above, with the exception of *Yayael,* which is now written, omitting the initial phoneme, as *Agiael.*

61. Here the text reads *Dimiuan;* in the following chapter, *Deminán.* In both cases, the second spelling will be used.

62. Thus in the text. *[A]conel* could be related to the verb *akonnabo* "to hear."

CHAPTER XI

*Concerning what happened to the four brothers when
they were fleeing from Yaya*

As soon as they reached Bayamanaco's door,[63] and they saw that he was
carrying *cazabe* [cassava bread],[64] the brothers said: "Ahiacabo guáro-
coel,"[65] which means: "Let us meet this our grandfather."[66] Likewise,
seeing his brothers before him, Deminán Caracaracol[67] went in to see if
he could get some cassava bread, which is the kind of bread they eat in
that country. Once inside Bayamanaco's house,[68] Caracaracol asked him
for *cazabe*, the aforesaid bread. And the latter put his hand on his nose
and spat a *guanguayo* [wad of spittle][69] onto his back; the *guanguayo* was
full of *cohoba*[70] that he had ordered prepared that day. This *cohoba* is a

63. Ulloa: *Bassamanaco*. The name will reappear in this same chapter written *Aiamauaco*
(note 68) and *Baiamanicoel* (note 72); in chapter XXV a chieftain named *Gamanacoel* (note
128) is mentioned. Writing the four spellings in columns gives us:

Ba	ss	a	m	a	n	a	c	o
[B]a	i	a	m	a	u	a	c	o
Ba	i	a	m	a	n	i	c	o	e	l
G[u]a	-	-	m	a	n	a	c	o	e	l

It is possible to infer that the *u* in *[B]aiamauaco* may have been an erroneous reading for *n*,
which often occurs in Ulloa, and that the *i* in the antepenultimate syllable of *Baiamanicoel*
corresponds to an *a*. As a result, *Bayamanaco* and *Bayamanacoel* are the forms that will be
used in this chapter, and *Guamanacoel* in chapter XXV. It may be helpful to add, in support of these spellings, that the Indians of an Orinoco tribe are called the *Tamanacos*.
64. Ulloa: *cazzabi;* Anghiera: *cazabi;* Las Casas vacillates between "*cazabi*, the penultimate
vowel long" (*Apologética historia*, chap. 10), and *caçabe* (chap. 59). The word, therefore, was
and continues to be paroxytone and not oxytone as some transcribers have accentuated it.
65. Ulloa: *Ahiacauo guarocoel.*
66. *Ahiacabo* corresponds to the Arawak *ajiaka ~ adiaka* "to speak, to say," and *guarocoel* to
wa-óroco-ti "our grandfather." See note 4 and also Douglas Taylor, "Some Remarks on the
Spelling and Formation of Taino Words," *International Journal of American Linguistics* 26
(1960), 347. Literally, it would be thus: "Let us speak with our grandfather."
67. Ulloa: *Deminan Caracaracol.*
68. Ulloa: *Aiamauaco.* For an explanation of the change in the form that has been chosen,
see note 63.
69. Ulloa: *guanguaio.* This word has lent itself to various interpretations. Anghiera translates it as "spit": "ut illi ex ictu sputi exortum." A Spanish version of the book by Fernando
(ed. Madrid, 1892, 1:292) gives: "he threw a squash on his back that was full of cohoba."
Edward G. Bourne translates it as "tobacco pouch"—that is to say, the little pouch for
keeping chopped tobacco (*Columbus*, p. 17). In the present context, Pietro Martire's conjecture seems the most accurate.
70. Ulloa: *cogioba;* Anghiera: *chohoba;* Las Casas: "These powders and these ceremonies or
acts were called *cohoba*, the middle syllable long." The said powder, according to the majority of commentators, was made by grinding dry tobacco leaves. Tobacco, however, does
not produce such hallucinatory effects. It must be, then, another plant, and Oviedo testi-

certain powder that they take at times to purge themselves and for other effects that will be described below. To take it, they use a reed half the length of an arm, and they put one end in the nose and the other in the powder; thus they inhale it through the nose, and this serves them as a great purgative. And in this way he gave them that *guanguayo* instead of the bread he was making, and he went away very indignant that they had asked him for it. . . . [71] After this, Caracaracol turned back to his brothers and told them what had happened to him with Bayamana-coel,[72] and how he spat *guanguayo* on his back, which ached very badly. Then his brothers looked at his back and saw it was very swollen; and that swelling grew so much that he was about to die. Then they tried to cut it, and they could not; and taking a stone axe, they opened it up, and a live, female turtle emerged; and so they built their house and raised the turtle.[73] I did not find out anymore about this, and what I have written down is of little help.

---

fies to this. In book 9 of the *Historia general y natural,* chapter 13 has the following title: "From the tree that in this region is thought to be *tharay* because it resembles it very much in its leaves, but on this Island Hispaniola they call it *cohoba.*" And in the text he adds: "And this *cohoba* has some peas the pods of which are a palm's width and more or less long, with some lentils as fruit that are not edible, and the wood is very good and strong." William E. Safford has identified the said tree as the *Piptadenia peregrina* ("Identity of the Cohoba, the Narcotic Snuff of Ancient Haiti," *Journal of the Washington Academy of Science* 6 (1916): 547–62). Carl O. Sauer corroborates the description of the plant in the information he offers: "Cohoba (*Piptadenia peregrina*), used as a narcotic snuff, mixed with tobacco, was probably introduced from South America" (*The Early Spanish Main* [Berkeley and Los Angeles, 1966], p. 56).

Cohoba has been reclassified as *Anadenanthera peregrina.* See Gerardo Reichel-Dolmatoff, *El chamán y el jaguar: Estudio de las drogas narcóticas entre los Indios de Colombia* [Mexico City, 1978], especially illustration 6 (between pages 160 and 161), glossary, p. 245, and bibliography, under Altschul, Siri von Reis.

This plant is known in the Dominican Republic as *tamarindo de teta* and in Puerto Rico as *cojóbana.*

Regarding the etymology, James Williams suggests that *cohoba* may be a word of Guaraní origin, composed of *cog* "to sustain, to fortify, to feed" and *hob* "leaf" ("Christopher Columbus and Aboriginal Indian Words," *Proceedings of the Twenty-Third International Congress of Americanists* [New York, 1930], p. 833).

71. A lacuna indicated in the text by an ellipsis.

72. Ulloa: *Baiamanicoel.* For an explanation of the change in the form that has been chosen, see note 63.

73. Anghiera changes the original version when he writes: "From the ulcer they say a woman was born, whom all the brothers used mutually, and upon her they engendered sons and daughters." This distortion can be rejected thanks to the evidence of an archaeological piece I located in the Museum of the American Indian, New York, which is clearly

And they also say that the Sun and the Moon emerged from a cave located in the country of a *cacique* named Mautiatihuel,[74] which cave is called Iguanaboina,[75] and they hold it in great esteem, and they have it all painted in their fashion, without any figures, with a lot of foliage and other such things. And in the said cave there were two zemis made from stone, small ones, the size of half an arm, with their hands tied, and they seemed to be sweating. They valued those zemis very highly; and when it did not rain, they say that they would go in there to visit them, and it would rain at once. And one zemi they called Boinayel,[76] and the other Márohu.[77]

CHAPTER XII

Concerning what they believe about the dead wandering about, and what they are like, and what they do

They believe there is a place where the dead go, which is called Coaybay,[78] and it is located on one side of the island, which is called So-

---

a turtle. A photographic reproduction of the piece can be seen in my edition of the *Historia de la invención de las Indias* by Hernán Pérez de Oliva [Bogotá, 1965], plate 8. See also José J. Arrom, *Mitología y artes prehispánicas de las Antillas* (Mexico City, 1975), p. 140, plates 56 and 57.

74. Ulloa: *Maucia Tiuuel;* Anghiera: *Machinnech.* It was likely one single word, *Mautia-ti-hu-el,* whose components — *maucia* or *mautia* "dawn, morning," *-ti,* nominalizing particle, *-hu,* sign of respect or veneration, and *-el* "son of"—would come to mean "Son-of-the-Dawn," or as if we were to say, the Chief or Lord of the Region of the Dawn. A coincidence: the Aztecs also worshiped the god they called *Tlahuizcalpan-tecuhtli,* "Lord of the House of the Dawn" (Alfonso Caso, *El pueblo del Sol* [Mexico, 1953], p. 53).

75. Ulloa: *Giououaua;* Anghiera: *Iouanaboina.* Both spellings tend toward the same form if one accepts the possibility that Ulloa may have once again confused the *n* and the *u* and that he skipped a syllable. The reading would then be *(G)Ioua-na-[boi]-na*—that is to say, the same as that of Pietro Martire. *Iouana* is the word that today is written *iguana.* And *boina* seems to be the same word *boiúna* that has been recorded in Amazon languages, meaning "brown serpent." See Luis Cámara Cascudo, *Diccionario de folclore brasileiro,* 2d ed. (Rio de Janeiro, 1962), pp. 123–24.

76. Ulloa: *Boinaiel;* Anghiera: *Binthaitel.* In accordance with the previous note, this *Boina-y-el* is the son of *Boina,* the Gray Serpent, a metaphor for rain-bearing clouds.

77. Ulloa: *Maroio;* Anghiera: *Marohu.* Pietro Martire's reading clearly records three morphemes: the privative prefix *ma-;* the root *-aro-* that appears in the Arawak words *or-aro, ur-aro, ul-aro* "cloud," and the nominalizing suffix *-hu,* which we have seen previously as a sign of reverence. It would mean, thus, "Without-Clouds," or Clear-Weather.

78. Ulloa: *Coaibai,* and thus in the remainder of the chapter, but *Comboi* in the following chapter. Pané declares, as he ends this paragraph, that it means "house and dwelling place of the dead." It corresponds, thus, to the *Cupay* of the Incas, *Mictlan* of the Aztecs, and *Xibalbá* of the Maya. See also notes 27 and 85.

raya.[79] They say that the first person in Coaybay was one who was called Maquetaurie Guayaba,[80] who was the lord of the said Coaybay, house and dwelling place of the dead.

CHAPTER XIII
Concerning the shape they say the dead have

They say that during the day they hide away, and at night they go out to walk about, and they eat a certain fruit that is called *guayaba*,[81] which has the flavor of [quince],[82] and in the daytime they are . . . ,[83] and at night they change into fruit, and they celebrate and accompany the living. And in order to recognize them, they observe this procedure: they touch one's belly with their hands, and if they do not find his navel, they say he is *operito*,[84] which means dead: that is why they say the dead have no navel. And thus they are sometimes fooled when they do not notice this,

79. Ulloa: *Soraia*. Carl F. von Martius records this word in a Latin-Arawak glossary and, attempting to guess its meaning, offers the translation "occasus solis" (*Beiträge*, p. 316). Perhaps it may have a more direct connection to the base -*ra*- "place, generally distant from the speaker," that enters into the composition of -*raia* "appearance" and from which are derived *ka-raia* "that which appears," *ti-raia* "appearance of things," and *ü-raia* "external aspect, vision" (Goeje, *The Arawak Language*, p. 143, para. 104a). In this case, *So-raia* would be related to the idea of a remote, inaccessible, unreal place—that is to say, a mythic place.

80. Ulloa: *Machetaurie Guaiaba*. *Maquetaurie* is perhaps related to the Arawak *kikke, kakü* "to live, life," which preceded by the privative *Ma*- would be the equivalent of "without-life." Within the American mythologies, it corresponds to the Aztec god *Mictlantecuhtli* "Lord of Mictlan, the dwelling of the disappeared." With respect to the relationship of the second word with the fruit of the same name, see note 81.

81. Ulloa: *guabazza*; Anghiera: *guannaba*, and thereafter he adds: "fructu nobis incognito cotono simili": fruit unknown to us similar to the quince. Antonio Bachiller y Morales thought that this fruit was the *guanábana* or soursop (*Cuba primitiva* [Havana, 1883], pp. 279–80). Bachiller's hypothesis has been accepted without question, including by Joan Corominas in his *Diccionario crítico etimológico de la lengua castellana* (Madrid, 1954, under *Guanábana*). However, the soursop (*Annona muricata* Lin.) bears no resemblance whatsoever to quince. It could be that the spelling *gua-nna-ba* represents rather a latinization of *guañaba, guanyaba*, or *guaiaba*, which in any case corresponds to the modern word *guayaba* (guava). The guava (*Psidium guayaba* Lin.) does indeed have a close resemblance to quince in shape, texture, and flavor. This interpretation is reinforced by the fact that the Lord of the Dwelling Place of the Dead was called, precisely, *Maquetaurie Guayaba*.

82. A lacuna indicated in the text by an ellipsis. The missing name is supplied from the quotation from Anghiera contained in note 81.

83. A lacuna indicated in the text by an ellipsis.

84. Ulloa: *operito*. This word, which Pané translates subsequently as "dead," is evidently related to *opía*. See the lines below in chapter XIII and notes 87 and 117.

and they lie with one of the Coaybay[85] women; when a man thinks he has her in his arms, he has nothing because the woman disappears in an instant. They still believe this even today. When a person is alive, they call his spirit *goeíza*,[86] and when he is dead, they call it *opía*.[87] They say this *goeíza* appears to them often, in a man's shape as well as a woman's, and they say there have been men who have wanted to do battle with it, and when such a man would lay his hands on it, it would disappear, and the man would put his arms elsewhere into some trees, and he would end up hanging from those trees. And everyone generally believes this, the children as well as the adults, and that it appears to them in the shape of father, mother, brothers, or relatives, and other forms. The fruit they say the dead eat is the size of a quince. And the aforesaid dead do not appear to them in the daytime, but always at night, and that is why one is very fearful who ventures to walk alone at night.

CHAPTER XIV

Concerning whence they deduce this and who leads them to hold such a belief

There are some men who are practitioners among them and are called *behiques*.[88] They practice many deceptions, as we shall relate below, to make the people believe that they speak with those [the dead] and know all their deeds and secrets, and that they take the illness away from them

---

85. Ulloa: *Comboi*. In the variants *Coaibai ~ Comboi*, the morpheme *baí ~ boí* seems to correspond to the forms *bahaí ~ bahü ~ bawhu* recorded in Arawak with the meaning "house," and to *boa ~ bouhí ~ bohío* recorded in Taíno with the same meaning. Regarding *coai*, it seems to be related to *kowa* "to be absent." In this case, *Coaybay* would be, as Pané indeed said, "house and dwelling place" of the absent ones, of the deceased.

86. Ulloa: *goeiz*. Brinton thinks that *goeíz* probably is a corruption of *guaíza* ("The Arawak Language," p. 438). Las Casas describes the *guaízas* as "very well-made masks" (*Historia de las Indias*, book I, chaps. 58, 62, 78, and 85), and he comments with regard to the pronunciation: "these faces or figures, which they called *guayças*, the letter *y* long" (*Apologética historia*, chap. 59). Because *ísiba* is "face, countenance," *wa-ísiba* would be "our face, our countenance."

87. Ulloa: *opia;* Las Casas: *hupía*. Both variants seem to correspond to the insular Carib *oupoye-m ~ opoye-m* "spirit" (Breton, *Dictionnaire*, p. 424).

88. Ulloa: *bohuti*, but it is transcribed *buhuitihu* in the following chapters with one exception, in chapter XIX, which reads *bihuitibu;* Anghiera: *bohitiios;* Las Casas vacillates between *bohique*, *behique*, and *behico;* Breton: *boyé* and *baydico;* in Guaraní *payé*. The Antillean writers of the Ciboneist School imposed the form *behique*, and it is this form that the Royal Academy has incorporated in its *Diccionario* (*Boletín de la Real Academia Española* 43, notebook 180 [January–April 1967], p. 82). We will use, thus, the authorized form and consign the variants to footnotes.

when they are sick; and thus they deceive them. Indeed, I have seen it in part with my own eyes, although of other matters I have told only what I heard from many people, particularly from the leaders, with whom I have had more contact than with others; indeed, they believe in these fables with greater certainty than the others. In fact, just as the Moors, they have their laws gathered in ancient songs,[89] by which they govern themselves, as do the Moors by their scripture. And when they wish to sing their songs, they play a certain instrument that is called *mayohabao*,[90] which is made of wood, hollow, strong, and very thin, the length of an arm and half an arm in width. The part that is played is made in the shape of a blacksmith's tongs, and the other part resembles a mace so that it looks like a long-necked squash. And they play this instrument, which has a voice so loud that it can be heard from a distance of a league and a half. To its sound they sing their songs, which they learn by heart, and the principal men play it; they learn to play it as children and to sing with it, according to their custom. Let us now move on to deal with many other matters concerning other ceremonies and customs of these heathen.

89. *Songs*. They were the *areítos*. Oviedo describes them in detail in the *Historia general y natural de las Indias*, book 5, chapter 1; Las Casas also describes them in the *Apologética historia*, chap. 204. The word *areíto* could be related to the verb *arit-ga*, which according to Breton means "se rappeler" (*Dictionnaire*, p. 53)—that is, "to remember, to recall."

Although it is often written *areito*, it should be *areíto*, with an accent on the *i*. Las Casas leaves no doubt as to the pronunciation: "*Areíto*, the *i* long" (*Historia de las Indias*, book 2, chap. 60).

90. Ulloa: *maiohauau*. Oviedo describes them without giving their name: "At times together with the song they mix a drum which is made from a round, hollow, concave piece of wood, as thick as a man and more or less as they wish to make it; and it sounds like the muffled drums the blacks make; but they do not put any leather on it, rather some holes and bands that cross over the hollow, hence it reverberates in a graceless fashion" (*Historia general*, book 5, chap. 1). And Las Casas does the same: "They were very fond of their dances, danced to the sound of the songs they sang and some raucous wooden drums, all made without leather or any attached thing" (*Apologética historia*, chap. 204). We have chosen *mayohabao* by analogy with *Arimao, Caonao, Cibao*, and other words of similar ending. The final *u* could have been an erroneous reading for *n*, and in that case it would be *mayohabán*. Some authors, when they modernize the term, write *mayohuacán*. I am not familiar with the original source that would justify this spelling.

CHAPTER XV

Concerning the observances of these Indian behiques,[91]
*and how they practice medicine and teach the people, and
in their medicinal cures they are often deceived*[92]
All or the majority of the people of the Island of Hispaniola have many zemis[93] of various sorts. Some contain the bones of their father and mother and relatives and ancestors; they are made of stone or of wood. And they have many of both kinds, some that speak, and others that cause the things they eat to grow, and others that make it rain, and others that make the winds blow. Those simple, ignorant people believe that those idols — or, more properly speaking, demons — make such things happen because they have no knowledge of our holy faith. When one of them is sick, they take him to the *behique*, who is the aforesaid physician. The physician is obliged to keep the same diet as the patient and to put on a sick face. This is done in the manner you will now see. He must also purge himself as the sick one does; and in order to purge themselves, they take a certain powder called *cohoba*,[94] inhaling it through the nose, which inebriates them in such fashion that they do not know what they are doing; and thus they say many senseless things, affirming therein that they are speaking with the zemis, and that the latter tell them that the sickness has come from them.

CHAPTER XVI
Concerning what the said behiques *do*
When they go to visit some sick man, before leaving the house, they take soot from the cooking pots or ground charcoal, and they blacken

91. Ulloa: *buhuitihu* and thus in the remaining instances with the exception indicated in note 88.
92. From the description Pané gives hereafter of the cures and ceremonies of the *behiques*, it will be apparent that they were in fact shamans. Regarding the existence of identical or similar ceremonies and beliefs among the Arawaks, Caribs, and other tribes of the Guianas, see Roth, *An Inquiry*, pp. 326-53, and C. H. de Goeje, "Philosophy, Initiation and Myths of the Indians of Guiana and Adjacent Countries," *Internationales Archiv für Ethnographie* 44 (1943): 60-94. Regarding the relationship between the practices of the *behiques* and shamanism, see Mircea Eliade, *Shamanism, Archaic Techniques of Ecstasy* (New York, 1964); Alfred Métraux, "Le shamanisme chez les Indiens de l'Amérique du Sud tropicale," *Acta Americana* 2 (1964): 197-219 and 320-41; and the articles by Claude Lévi-Strauss, "The Sorcerer and His Magic" and "The Effectiveness of Symbols," included in his *Structural Anthropology* (New York, 1967), pp. 161-201.
93. Ulloa: *cimini.*
94. The text now gives *cohoba* (see note 70).

their faces entirely so as to make the sick man believe whatever they may wish about his illness; and then they pick up some little bones and a bit of meat. And wrapping all this up in something so it will not scatter, the physician puts it into his mouth; at this time the sick man has already been purged with the powder as we have said. Once the physician is inside the sick man's house, he sits down, and everyone falls silent; and if there are children, they send them outside so they will not hinder the work of the *behique,* nor do more than one or two of the most preeminent persons remain in the house. And being thus alone, they take some *güeyo* herbs[95] . . . wide, and another herb, wrapped in an onion leaf, a half palm in length; and one of the said *güeyos*[96] is what they all share, and after tearing them into pieces with their hands, they knead them; and then they put them in their mouths so as to vomit what they have eaten so it will do them no harm. Then they begin to intone the aforesaid song; and lighting a torch, they drink that juice. When this first part is done, after remaining still for a time, the *behique* stands up and goes toward the sick man, who is seated alone in the middle of the house, as has been said, and he walks around him twice, as he deems appropriate; and then he stands in front of him and takes him by the legs, touching him on the thighs and continuing down to the feet; then he pulls hard on him, as if he wished to pull something out. From there he goes to the exit of the house and closes the door, and he speaks, saying: "Go away to the forest, or to the sea, or wherever you wish." And with a puff, like one who blows into a straw, he turns one more time, puts his hands together and closes his mouth; and his hands tremble, like when one is very cold, and he blows on his hands and sucks in his breath, like when one sucks the marrow of a bone, and he sucks on the sick man's neck or on his stomach or on his back or on his cheeks, or on his chest, or on his belly or on many parts of his body. When this is done, he begins to cough and to make ugly faces, as if he had eaten some bitter thing, and he spits into his hand and takes out those things we have already told he put into his mouth while in his own house or on his way to the sick man, whether stone or bone or meat, as has already been said. And if it is something to eat, he says to the sick man: "You must know that you have eaten something that has provoked in you the illness you are suffering; look how I have taken it out of your body, for your zemi had put it into your body because you did not pray to him or

95. Ulloa: *gioia* "jewel," followed by a lacuna indicated by an ellipsis. The Italian word *gioia* is an erroneous reading of the Taíno word that in chapter XVII is transcribed *gueio* (see note 100).
96. Ulloa: *gioie* "jewels."

you did not build him some temple, or you did not give him some land." And if it is made of stone, he says to the sick man: "Keep it with care." And sometimes they believe it is true that those stones are good, and they help women give birth, and they keep them very carefully, wrapped in cotton, putting them into small baskets, and they feed them some of what they eat, and they do the same thing with the zemis [97] they have at home. On a solemn occasion, when they have an abundance of food, fish, meat, or bread, or whatever else, they put some of everything in the house of the zemi [98] so that the said idol may eat from those things. The next day they take all these foodstuffs to their homes, after the zemi has eaten. And so may God help them if the zemi eats any of those things because the zemi is a dead thing, shaped from stone or made of wood.

CHAPTER XVII

How the aforesaid physicians have at times been deceived
When the sick man dies even after the aforesaid things have been done, if the dead person has many relatives or is the lord of a village and can confront the said *behique*, which means physician [99] — for those who have little power do not dare to contend with these physicians — on those who wish to do the *behique* harm do the following: wanting to know if the sick man has died through the fault of the physician or because he did not keep the diet as the physician ordered, they take an herb that is called *güeyo*,[100] which has thick, long leaves similar to those of the basil plant and is also known by the name of *zacón*.[101] They extract the juice of the leaf, and they cut the dead person's nails and the hair on his forehead, and they grind it to dust between two stones; this they mix with the juice of the said herb, and they give it to the dead man to drink through the mouth or through the nose, and while they are doing this, they ask the dead man if the physician was the cause of his death and

97. Ulloa: *cimini*.
98. Here *cimiche* and thus in the two following instances.
99. *Physician*. Las Casas amplifies the concept when he writes: "Indeed, these priests, who are called *behiques* in the language of these islands and who were their theologians, prophets, and soothsayers, practiced some deceptions upon these people, primarily when they acted as physicians."
100. Ulloa: *gueio*. Regarding *güeyo*, Fernando Ortiz writes: "Among the Indians of the Guianas tobacco is generally chewed, for which purpose it is mixed with certain salty-tasting ashes obtained from a species of alga (*Mourera fluvialis*, Aubl.) they gather near river cascades, an alga the Indians call *weya*" (*Contrapunteo del tabaco y el azúcar*, 2d ed. [Havana, 1963], p. 176). See also Walter E. Roth, *An Introductory Study of the Arts, Crafts and Customs of the Guiana Indians* (Washington, 1924), p. 242.
101. Ulloa: *zachon*.

if he kept the diet. And they ask him this many times until at last he speaks as clearly as if he were alive so that he finally answers everything they ask him, saying that the *behique* did not keep the diet or that he was the cause of his death that time. And they say that the physician asks him if he is alive and how he speaks so clearly, and he answers that he is dead. And after they have found out what they want, they return him to the grave from whence they took him in order to find out from him what we have said. They also work the aforementioned spells in another fashion in order to find out what they want: they take the dead man, and they make a great fire, like that with which the collier makes coal, and when the wood has burned down to coals, they throw the dead man into that great bonfire and then cover him with earth, like the collier covers charcoal, and there they let him stay for as long as they deem appropriate. And while he is there in that fashion, they question him as has been told above: he answers that he knows nothing. And they ask him this ten times, and thereafter he speaks no more. They ask him if he is dead, but he does not speak more than these ten times.

CHAPTER XVIII
How the relatives of the dead man take revenge when
they have got an answer by means of the spell of the drinks
One day the relatives of the dead man gather and wait for the aforesaid *behique,* and they beat him so soundly that they break his legs and arms and head, clubbing him all to pieces, and they leave him thus, believing they have killed him. And they say that at night many snakes come, of various kinds, white, black, and green, and of many other colors, and they lick the face and the whole body of the said physician whom they left for dead, as we have said.[102] He is in this state for two or three days, and while he is thus, the bones of his legs and arms join once again and mend, they say, and he stands up and walks a little and goes back to his house. And those who see him inquire, asking: "Were you not dead?"

102. For the proper elucidation of this paragraph, it may be worthwhile to mention a coincidence with the Aztec religion. In the esoteric language of the ancient Mexican priests, "pains are called 'serpents' and they are of four colors, so as to connect them to the cardinal points. There is the blue serpent, the yellow serpent, the red one and the white one" (Caso, *El pueblo,* p. 111). It could well have been that Pané understood literally what the Indians told him in metaphors and that the expressions "clubbing him [the *behique*] to pieces" until they "leave him thus, believing they have killed him" were hyperboles—as they are in Spanish. One may note a few lines after these phrases that the *behique* did not die from the beating: "if they can catch him again, they take out his eyes and smash his testicles because they say that none of these physicians can die, however much they may beat him."

But he answers that the zemis[103] went to his aid in the shape of serpents. And when they see him alive, the relatives of the dead man are very annoyed because they believed they had avenged the death of their relative, and they become desperate and try to lay their hands on him so as to kill him; and if they can catch him again, they take out his eyes and smash his testicles because they say that none of these physicians can die, however much they may beat him, if they do not remove his testicles.

[CHAPTER XVIII BIS]
How they find out what they want from the one whom
they have burned, and how they take revenge
When they uncover the fire, the smoke that comes out rises up until it is lost from sight, and it makes a crackling sound when it comes out of the fire pit. Then it comes back down and enters into the house of the *behique* physician, and he falls ill at that very instant if he did not keep the diet, and he becomes covered with wounds, and his whole body peels. And they take this as a sign that he has not kept it, and that is why the sick man died. Therefore, they try to kill him, as has already been told. These are, thus, the sorceries they are in the habit of working.

CHAPTER XIX
How they make and keep the zemis made of wood or of stone
The ones of wood[104] are made in this way: when someone is walking along, and he says he sees a tree that is moving its roots, the man very fearfully stops and asks it who it is. And it answers him: "Summon me[105] a *behique*,[106] and he will tell you who I am." And when that man goes to the aforesaid physician, he tells him what he has seen. And the sorceror or wizard runs at once to see the tree of which the other man has told him; he sits next to it and prepares *cohoba*[107] for it, as we have related earlier in the story of the four brothers. Once the *cohoba* is made,

103. Here the text reads *cimini*. As the variants of this term have now been indicated, they will not be mentioned henceforth.
104. The text reads *di sasso* "of stone." The passage that follows makes it apparent that it should have been *di legno* "of wood."
105. In the text: "lo mi chiamo" or "I am called." An erroneous translation of what should in Spanish have read: "Llámame" (call me). This correction is confirmed by Las Casas, who writes in the corresponding section: "Summon me here a *behique*, and he will tell you who I am."
106. In the text, changing the unusual spelling: *bihuitihu*.
107. In the text: *cogioba* and thus in the remainder of the chapter. Regarding these variants, the identification of the plant and a possible etymology of the name, see note 70.

he stands up and tells it all his titles, as if they were those of a great lord, and he asks it: "Tell me who you are, and what you are doing here, and what you wish from me, and why you have had me summoned. Tell me if you want to be cut down, or if you want to come with me, and how you want to be carried, for I will build you a house with land." Then that tree or zemi, turned into an idol or devil, answers him, telling him the manner in which he wants it to be done. And he cuts it and fashions it in the manner he has been ordered; he constructs its house with land, and many times during the year he prepares *cohoba* for it. That *cohoba* is used to pray to it and to please it and to ask and find out from the afore-said zemi good and bad things and also to ask it for riches. And when they want to find out if they will achieve victory over their enemies, they enter into a house in which none but the leading men enter. And their lord is the first one who begins to prepare *cohoba*, and he plays an instrument; and while he is making the *cohoba*, none of those who are in his company speaks until the lord has finished. After he has finished his prayer, he stays awhile with his head lowered and his arms on his knees; then he lifts his head, looking toward the heavens, and he speaks. Then they all answer him aloud in unison; and after all have spoken, they give thanks, and he relates the vision he has had, inebriated from the *cohoba* he has inhaled through his nose and that has gone to his head. And he says he has spoken with the zemi and that they will achieve victory, or their enemies will flee, or there will be a great loss of life, or wars or hunger or another such thing, according to what he, who is drunk, may relate of what he remembers. You may judge in what state his brain may be, for they say they think they see the houses turn upside down, with their foundations in the air, and the men walk on foot toward the heavens. And they prepare this *cohoba* not only for the zemis of stone and of wood, but also for the bodies of the dead, as we have related above.

The stone zemis are of different constructions. There are some they say the physicians take out[108] of their bodies, and the sick maintain that those are the best ones to make pregnant women give birth. There are others that speak; they have the shape of a thick turnip with their leaves spread out on the ground and long like those of the caper bush. Their leaves are in general similar to those of the elm tree; others have three points, and they believe they cause the *yuca* [cassava] to sprout.[109] They have a root similar to the radish. The leaf of the *yuca*[110] has at most six or seven points; I do not know to what it might be compared because I

108. The text reads: *seccano,* an error for *saccano.*
109. The text reads: *giuca.*
110. The text reads: *giutola.* In the references that follow, it is again written *giuca.*

have not seen anything like it in Spain or any other country. The stalk of the *yuca* is as tall as a man. Let us now speak of the belief they have concerning their idols and zemis, and how they are greatly deceived by them.

CHAPTER XX
Concerning the zemi Buya and Aiba,[111] who they say was burned when there was war, and afterwards, when they washed him with yuca juice, he grew arms, and his eyes reappeared, and his body grew

Yuca was small, and they washed him with water and the aforesaid juice so that he would be large; and they affirm that he brought diseases to those who had made that zemi because they had not taken him *yuca* to eat. This zemi is called Baibrama.[112] And when someone fell ill, they would call the *behique* and ask him where his illness came from, and he would answer that Baibrama had sent it to him because they had not sent those who were in charge of caring for his house with anything for him to eat. And this is what the *behique* said the zemi Baibrama had told him.

CHAPTER XXI
Concerning Guamarete's[113] zemi

They say that when they built the house of Guamarete, who was a preeminent man, they placed there a zemi that he kept on the top of his

---

111. Ulloa: *Bugia et Aiba*. The lack of subject-verb agreement with the rest of the sentence could be due to the fact that *buya* and *aiba* appear to be epithets rather than the name of the zemi: they mean, in Tupí, "ugly" and "bad." (See Brinton, "The Arawak Language," p. 444, and also Stradelli, *Vocabularios*, under *ayua* and *puxi*, pp. 385 and 625 respectively.) This myth is perhaps related to the domestication of cassava and the discovery of the process to eliminate the poison from the juice of the bitter cassava. As is known, when the juice is boiled, the toxic substance—prussic acid—evaporates, and a thick broth is left that serves as a condiment for food and cassava bread.

112. Ulloa: *Baidrama;* Las Casas: "Vaybrama, the penultimate syllable long." One may note that now the name of the zemi is given, in the singular, instead of the epithets previously mentioned. Regarding this zemi, Las Casas writes: "They said the zemi . . . had been burned in a war they had waged, and when they washed him with the juice of the root that we said above was called *yuca* [cassava], from which they made cassava bread, he grew arms, and his eyes reappeared, and his body grew; and because *yuca* or the aforesaid root was very small in those days, after they washed it with *yuca* water, it was henceforth, as it now is, fat and very large. This zemi brought diseases to men." If *bai ~ vay* is the Arawak *bahai ~ bahü* "house" (see note 85), Baibrama could perhaps have been a protecting god related to the home and the domestication and consumption of cassava.

113. Ulloa: *Guamorete;* Anghiera: *Guamaretus*. If the third vowel was *o, Guamorete* could correspond to the Arawak *Wa murreti* "Our Creator"; if it was an *a*, the name would correspond to *wama*, "señor" (lord), or as Pané explains, "a prominent man." I opt, thus, for Anghiera's spelling.

house; this zemi was called Corocote.[114] And once when they were at war among themselves, Guamarete's enemies burned the house in which the aforesaid zemi Corocote was located. They say he got up then and walked the distance of a crossbow shot away from that place, next to some water. And when he was on top of the house, they say, he would come down at night and lie with the women; and afterwards Guamarete died, and the aforesaid zemi fell into the hands of another *cacique*, and he kept on lying with the women. And they said further that two crowns sprang from his head, which is why they are in the habit of saying: "Because he has two crowns, he is surely the son of Corocote." And they hold this to be very true indeed. Another *cacique*, called Guatabanex,[115] had this zemi later, and his place is called Jacagua.[116]

CHAPTER XXII
Concerning another zemi called Opiyelguobirán,[117] *which was in the possession of a preeminent man called Sabananiobabo,*[118] *who had many subjects under his command*
The zemi Opiyelguobirán has four feet, like a dog, they say, and is made of wood, and often at night he leaves the house and goes into the jungle.

114. Ulloa: *Corocote;* Anghiera: *Corochotus.* It could be the same as the Arawak word *korrokori* "gold, reddish metal," or the Guaraúno word *corucuri* "bronze."
115. Ulloa: *Guatabanex.* Here the *b* seems to have represented, as in the case discussed in note 116, the vocalic value of our modern *u:* today we would read *Guatauanex* or *Guataguanex.* Las Casas mentions a *cacique* from the Magdalena called *Guatiguaná* (*Historia de las Indias,* book 1, chap. 104). Perhaps these are different spellings of the same name.
116. Ulloa: *Giacaba.* In the transcription of this toponym, the *b* has the vocalic value of the *u: Jacaua* or *Jacagua.* In the Dominican Republic, there is a place called *Jacagua,* located precisely near Santiago de los Caballeros, the area where Pané gathered this data (Emilio Tejera, *Palabras indijenas de la isla de Santo Domingo* [Santo Domingo, 1951], p. 314). There is also in Cuba a place named *Jacagua* (Vivanco, *El lenguaje,* p. 123), and in Puerto Rico there is the River Jacagua, near Ponce. We have elected to write the word, therefore, in accordance with the oral tradition.
117. Ulloa: *Opigielguouiran;* Anghiera: *Epileguanita. Opiyel* seems to be related to the Taíno *opía ~ hupía,* insular Carib *opoye-m.* (See notes 84 and 87.) With regard to *guobirán gu[a]* seems to be the pronominal prefix *wa,* "our," and *-obirán* is perhaps related to *Oroán,* which Goeje records in Akawai with the meaning of "Spirit of the Darkness" (*The Arawak Language,* p. 199, para. 166f).
118. Ulloa: *Cauauaniouaua.* When Ulloa transcribed the first letter, he appears to have forgotten the cedilla in what should have read *çabana;* that is the spelling generally found in the documents of the period for the word that later was written *zabana* and today *sabana. Iouaua* would give *iobaba* and more properly *jobabo. Jobabo* is the name of a river and a city in Cuba and also of other places in the Antilles. *Sabana-n-iobabo* is equivalent to Sabana of the Jobabal or of the Jobos.

They went to look for him there, and when they brought him home, they would tie him up with rope, but he would return to the jungle. And they tell that when the Christians arrived on the Island of Hispaniola, this zemi escaped and went into a lagoon; and they followed his tracks as far as the lagoon, but they never saw him again, nor did they hear anything about him.[119] As I buy, so also do I sell.

CHAPTER XXIII

Concerning another zemi whose name was Guabancex[120]
This zemi Guabancex was in the country of a great *cacique*, one of the principal *caciques*, whose name was Aumatex.[121] This zemi is a woman, and they say there are two others in her company; one is a herald, and the other a gatherer and governor of the waters. And they say that when Guabancex grows angry, she moves the wind and water and tears down the houses and uproots the trees. They say this zemi is a woman and is made of stones from that country. Of the other two zemis in her company, one is called Guataubá[122] and is a crier or herald who on orders from Guabancex commands all the other zemis from that province to assist in causing a great deal of wind and rain. The other is called Coatrisquie,[123] who they say gathers the waters in the valleys between the mountains and afterwards lets them run to ravage the country. And they hold this to be true.

119. Paul Barker and Gerard Goyot identify this god with an archaeological piece that is in no way related to the image of a dog: "Le chien de pierre de Chansolme, 'Opigiel-gourian,' dieu des Tainos" (*Bulletin du Bureau d'Ethnologie*, Port-au-Prince, July 30, 1964, 56 pp.). On the other hand, I have located an image in wood, just as Pané describes it, in the Smithsonian Institution, Washington, D.C. I have reproduced it in the cited edition of the *Historia de la invención de las Indias*, plate 5, and in my *Mitología y artes prehispánicas en las Antillas*, p. 100.
120. Thus in the text.
121. Thus in the text. This "great *cacique*" was perhaps a mythical being and not a historical person. On the other hand, there is evidence of the existence of a *cacique* of scant importance whose name appears transcribed as *Amanex* ("Repartimiento de la isla Española," in *Collección de documentos inéditos relativos a . . . América y Oceanía*, 1:67).
122. Ulloa: *Guatauua*. *Gua-* could be the pronominal prefix *wa* "our." Because the *b* in Taíno corresponds to a *p* in other languages related to Taíno, *Taubá* could be the same as *Tupá* or *Tupán*, god of thunder among the Tupí-Guaraní people and among some tribes of the Guianas (see Goeje, "Philosophy, Initiation," pp. 41 and 71).
123. Ulloa: *Coatrischie*. Although there is a certain resemblance between the name *Coatrisquie* and that of the Aztec goddess *Coatlicue*, the functions of Coatrisquie correspond rather to those of Chalchiuhtlicue, sister of Tláloc and goddess of the waters. I suspect that it may be a question of a simple paronymy.

CHAPTER XXIV

Concerning what they believe about another zemi whose name was Baraguabael[124]

This zemi belongs to a principal *cacique* of the Island of Hispaniola and is an idol; they attribute various names to him, and he was found in the manner you will now hear. They say that in times past before the island was discovered, they do not know how long ago, as they were hunting one day, they happened upon a certain animal. They ran after it, and it fled into a hole; and as they searched for it, they saw a log that seemed to be a living thing. Thus when the hunter saw this, he ran to his lord, who was *cacique* and father of Guaraionel,[125] and told him what he had seen. Then they went there and found the thing as the hunter had said; and having taken that trunk, they built him a house. They say that he left that house three times, and he would go to the place from where they had taken him, not to the very same place but rather one nearby. Therefore, the aforesaid lord, or his son Guaraionel, ordered him to be sought; they found him hiding, and they tied him up again and put him in a sack. And in spite of all this, tied up as he was, he would go off as before. And those ignorant people hold this to be a very certain thing indeed.

CHAPTER XXV

Concerning the things they affirm were told by two principal caciques of the Island of Hispaniola, one called Cacibaquel,[126] *father of the aforesaid Guarionex,*[127] *and the other Guamanacoel*[128]

And as they all commonly do, Cáicihu[129] held a fast to the honor of

124. Ulloa: *Faraguuaol.* The sound represented here by *f* is also generally represented by *b* or *p* (Goeje, *The Arawak Language,* pp. 110 ff.), perhaps it is more properly *Baraguabael.* Written thus, it would be related to *Baraguá* (a place in Cuba between Santiago and Holguín) and to *Baracoa, Barajagua,* and other toponyms in which *bara* means "sea." This restoration, in spite of its conjectural nature, would at least be consistent with what has survived of the Taíno language.

125. Ulloa: *Guaraionel,* and thus it appears again in the chapter. In chapter XXV, it appears as *Guarionel,* then *Guarionex,* and on one occasion *Guarionés.* Las Casas and other chroniclers always write *Guarionex.* The first variant suggests the possibility that the name was originally *Waraúno-el* "from the lineage of the guaraúnos."

126. Ulloa: *Cazziuaquel. Cazziba* may be the same root seen in *Cacibajagua* with the meaning of "cave" or "cavern" (note 10); *-quel* is perhaps composed of the infix *(e)-que,* "shelter" or "refuge," and *el,* "descendent of."

127. Here the text reads: *Guarionel.* See notes 148 and 153.

128. Here the text reads: *Gamanacoel.* The name of this *cacique* seems to be related to the Bayamanacoel who appears in chapter XI. See Notes 63, 68, and 72.

129. Ulloa: *Caizzihu.* Basing his work on the data of the cartographer Andrés de Morales,

that great lord they say is in heaven, as is written in the beginning of this book. For the fast they retreat for six or seven days without eating anything except the juice of the herbs with which they also bathe.[130] When this time is over, they begin to eat something to give them sustenance. And during the time they have been without eating, because of the weakness they feel in their bodies and in their heads, they say they have seen something perhaps desired by them. Thus they all hold that fast in honor of their zemis to find out if they will achieve victory over their enemies, to acquire riches or whatever they wish for.

And they say this *cacique* affirmed he had spoken with Yucahuguamá,[131] who had told him that those who remained alive after his death would enjoy their dominion for but a brief time because a clothed people would come to their land who would overcome them and kill them, and they would die of hunger. But at first they thought those people must be the cannibals;[132] but later, considering that the cannibals did nothing more than steal and flee, they believed the zemi must be referring to other people. Thus they now believe the Admiral and his people are the ones.

Anghiera describes a region of Hispaniola called *Caizcimú*. And he explains: "The beginning of the island on the east includes the province of *Caizcimú*, said in this way because in their language *cimú* means 'front or beginning'" (*Decada* 3, book 7, chap. 3). In Cuba there are also several places that have the name *Caisimú* (Vivanco, *El lenguaje*, p. 46). In this toponym, it is likely that *cai* corresponds to the Arawak *cay ~ cairi* "island," today Hispanicized as *cayo* (key).

130. The plant earlier called *digo* (see chapter II, note 17). It is not known with any certainty what plant this *digo* could have been. Although he does not mention the plant by this name, Las Casas says in chapter 167: "They would fast for four months and more at one stretch, without eating anything except only a certain juice of an herb or herbs. . . . And this is the same coca that is so esteemed in the provinces of Peru, as we know from the testimony of the clerics and of the Indians who have come from Peru, who saw it and first became acquainted with it on the aforesaid Island of Cuba and in great abundance." If it was not coca, at least it would have been a plant whose effects were similar to those of coca.

131. Ulloa: *Giocauuaghama;* Las Casas: *Yocahuguama*. Las Casas's transcription, written directly in Spanish, is the most authoritative. It corresponds to the words *Yúcahu* "Ser-de-la-yuca" and *guamá* (in Arawak *wama* "lord"). This Lord of the Yucca must be the same Yúcahu Bagua Maórocoti mentioned in chapter V, note 4.

132. Ulloa: *canibali,* Anghiera: *canibalibus. Caníbal* (cannibal) and *caribe* (Carib) are correlatives of the same indigenous word. In the *Diario del primer viaje*, Columbus transcribes *caníbales* (November 23), *caniba* (November 26), and *caribes* (December 26). Las Casas, commenting upon Pané's remarks, writes: "Those people must have been those whom we call Caribs, and at that time they called them and we called them cannibals." From this commentary I infer that Pané wrote *cannibals;* I respect, thus, his spelling, but clarify that they were really the Caribs.

Here I want to relate what I have seen and experienced when I and other brothers were going to go to Castille. And I, Fray Ramón, a humble friar, remained behind, and I went to the Magdalena,[133] a fortress built by Don Christopher Columbus, Admiral, Viceroy, and Governor of the Islands and the Mainland of the Indies, by order of our lords King Ferdinand and Queen Isabella. When I was at that fortress, in the company of its commander, Artiaga,[134] under orders from the aforesaid Governor Don Christopher Columbus, God was pleased to illumine with the light of the holy Catholic faith an entire household of leading citizens of the said province of the Magdalena, which province was then called Macorís,[135] and the lord of it was named Guanáoboconel,[136] which means son of Guanáobocon.[137] His household included his servants and favorites, who are called *naborías*,[138] and there were sixteen people altogether, all relatives, among whom there were five brothers. One of these died, and the other four received the holy baptismal water; and I believe they died as martyrs because of what was seen in their death and steadfastness. The first to be killed and to receive the holy baptismal water was an Indian named Guatícaba,[139] who later took the name of Juan. He was the first Christian who suffered a cruel death, and I am certain he died a martyr.[140] For I have learned from some who

133. Ulloa: *Maddalena.* Las Casas explains: "The Admiral had already ordered two fortresses built, one that he called the Magdalena . . . three or four leagues or a little more from where the town of Santiago is located at present" (*Historia de las Indias*, book 1, chap. 110; in the Mexico City edition, 1951, vol. 1, p. 429).

134. Luis de Artiaga (Las Casas, *Historia de las Indias*, book 1, chap. 110).

135. Ulloa: *Maroris.* Las Casas: *Macorix.* Its modern spelling is *Macorís.* Regarding its meaning, see note 147.

136. Ulloa: *Guauaouoconel.* Las Casas: *Guanaoconel. Guanabo* has survived in numerous Antillean toponyms: that of a beach near Havana, for example. And, one may remember, we have already met a mythical person "called Conel, who was mute" (chapter X, Note 62).

137. Ulloa: *Guauaenechin.* I change the reading to *Guanáobocon* so that it will correspond to the spelling of the previous name. I should point out, however, that the reading *Guanáenequen* could be equally valid.

138. Ulloa: *giahuuauariù;* when a word reappears that could very well be the same term (chapter XXVI, note 160), it is written *Gianauuariù.* Both in *yahu-nab(u)ariù* and in *Ya(hu)-nabuariù,* the cluster *nab(u)ariù ~ nabuariù* "servant" should be the same *(n)aboría* given a few lines below in the chapter (see note 141). Because the form *naboría* is the one most generally given in the documents of the Indies and the one accepted by the Royal Academy, I have chosen that spelling.

139. Ulloa: *Guaticaua.* He will mention him again in this chapter as *Guaicauanú* (see note 150). Supplying the missing letters in brackets, *Gua-tí-ca-ba[nu]* and *Gua-[t]í-ca-ba-nu* are the same name.

140. Las Casas gives a very different version of the cause of the death of this person. See appendix C, chapter 167, penultimate paragraph.

were present at his death that he said: "Dios naboría daca, Dios naboría daca,"[141] which means "I am a servant of God." And in this manner his brother Antón[142] died as well, and with him another, pronouncing the same words as he. All those of this household and people were in my company to do whatever pleased me. Those who remained alive and are still living today are Christians by the work of the aforesaid Don Christopher Columbus, Viceroy and Governor of the Indies, and now by the grace of God there are many more Christians.

Let us now speak of what happened to us in the province of the Magdalena.[143] When I was in the aforesaid Magdalena, the said Lord Admiral arrived to relieve Artiaga[144] and some Christians under seige by the enemy, subjects of a principal *cacique* called Caonabó.[145] The Lord Admiral told me then that the language spoken in the province of the Magdalena [or] Macorís[146] was different from the other one and was not understood throughout the country.[147] Nonetheless, I should go to live with another principal *cacique* called Guarionex,[148] lord of many people, because his language was understood throughout the land. Thus, by his command, I went to live with the said Guarionex. And it is indeed true that I said to the Lord Governor Christopher Columbus: "Sir, how is

141. Ulloa: *Dio aboriadacha, Dio aboriadacha.* Las Casas corrects thus: " 'Dios naboría daca, Dios naboría daca,' which means in the most common and most universal language of this island, 'I am a servant of God. . . . *Naboría* means 'servant or manservant' and *daca* means 'I.' " *Daca*, indeed, corresponds to *dA-*, a pronominal prefix, first person singular, in Lokono and other Arawak languages. With regard to *naboría*, Douglas Taylor says the following: "One would also like to find a meaning for Taíno *naboría*, said to designate the lowest caste or class; and if Lokono *budia*, glossed by Goeje as 'small remnant' may be translated 'remainder, rest', it seems not unlikely that this Taíno word should contain a cognate of the Lokono stem together with Lokono and Guajiro *nA-* 'they, their, them' " ("Some Remarks," p. 348).

142. Ulloa: *Antonio.* Las Casas, writing in Spanish, records: "Another called Antón, who was his brother." Consequently, the abbreviated form authorized by Las Casas has been used here.

143. Ulloa: "isola della Madalena." An evident confusion; it was not an island but a province. See a few lines below in the chapter and also note 146.

144. Ulloa: *Ariaga*, in error for *Artiaga*.

145. Ulloa: *Caouabo*. This is, of course, Caonabó. I write *Caonabó*, with the oxytone accentuation, following the testimony of Las Casas: "The fourth king was Caonabó, the last syllable long" (*Apologética historia*, book 3, chap. 197).

146. Ulloa: *Maddalena Maroris*.

147. Las Casas explains: "It was called Macorix in the most universal of the Indian languages of this island, almost like a strange and barbarous language, because the universal tongue was the most polished and regular or clear, according to what we said in the description of this island, written above in Chapters 90 and 91" (*Historia de las Indias*, book 1, chap. 110).

148. Here the text reads: *Guarionex*.

it that Your Lordship wishes me to go to live with Guarionex, knowing no language other than that of Macorís? Let Your Lordship grant leave for some of the Nuhuirey[149] people, who later became Christians and knew both languages, to accompany me." He granted this request and told me to take with me whoever pleased me. And God in his goodness gave me for company the best of the Indians, and the one who was most tutored in the holy Catholic faith; and afterwards he took him from me. Praise be to God who gave him to me and then took him from me. Truly I considered him a good son and brother; he was Guatícabanu,[150] who afterwards became a Christian and was called Juan.

Of the things that happened to us there, I, a humble friar, will relate a few, and of how Guatícabanu and I left and went to Isabela, and there we waited for the Lord Admiral until he returned from lifting the siege of the Magdalena. And as soon as he arrived, we went to where the Lord Governor had sent us, in the company of a man by the name of Juan de Ayala,[151] who was in charge of a fortress the aforesaid Governor Christopher Columbus had ordered built a half league from the place where we were to reside. And the Lord Admiral ordered the aforesaid Juan de Ayala to give us food from all the stores there were in the fortress, which fortress was called La Concepción. Consequently we were with that *cacique* Guarionex almost two years, always teaching him our holy faith and the customs of the Christians. In the beginning he showed us goodwill and gave us hope that he would do whatever we wished and that he wanted to be a Christian, saying that we should teach him the Pater Noster, the Ave María, and the Creed and all the other prayers and things that pertain to a Christian. And so he learned the Pater Nos-

149. Ulloa: *Nuhuirci.* This word, written in this fashion, does not sound Antillean. In the first syllable, the vowel seems to have been *a* instead of *u:* in that same geographical location, both a place and a river are called *Nagua* (Emilio Tejera, *Indigenismos* [Santo Domingo, 1977], 2:1086); in the last syllable, he probably read *c* where it may perhaps have been *e.* The name would then be *Nahuirey* or perhaps *Nagüirey*, with an ending in *ey*, frequent in Taíno in many common nouns (*batey, caney, carey, mamey, yarey*) and in numerous toponyms (*Camagüey, Higüey*). See also note 38 regarding another case in which Ulloa read *c* where it ought to have been *e.*

150. Here *Guaicauanú* and likewise a few lines below in the chapter. Regarding the correction, see note 139.

151. Ulloa: *Giouanni di Agiada.* Las Casas (book 1, chap. 110) explains: "The other fortress was built in the province and kingdom of Guarionex, 15 or a few more leagues away on the same *La Vega,* farther to the east of the other one, where later the city was populated that was and is called Concepción. . . . In this fortress he placed as commander a nobleman by the name of Juan de Ayala." The city was later named Concepción de la Vega Real; today it is La Vega.

ter and the Ave María and the Creed, and likewise many members of his household learned them; and every morning he would say his prayers and made those of his household say them twice. But afterwards he grew angry, and he abandoned his good intention; other leaders of that land were to blame, for they reproached him because he wanted to obey the law of the Christians, because the Christians were wicked and had taken possession of their lands by force. Therefore, they advised him not to deal further with Christian matters, but rather to come to an agreement and conspire to kill the Christians because they could not satisfy the Christians, and they had resolved absolutely not to do what they want. Because he retreated from his good intention, and seeing that Guarionex was retreating and abandoning what we had taught him, we decided to leave and go where we might gather better fruit, teaching the Indians and indoctrinating them in the matters of the holy faith. And thus we went to another principal *cacique* who showed us goodwill, saying he wanted to be a Christian. That *cacique* was called Mabiatué.[152]

[CHAPTER XXV BIS]
How we left to go to the country of the aforesaid Mabiatué—that is, I, Fray Ramón Pané, a humble friar, Fray Juan de Borgoña of the Order of Saint Francis, and Juan Mateo, the first man to receive the holy baptismal water on the Island of Hispaniola
On the second day after we had left the village and residence of Guarionex[153] to go to another *cacique* called Mabiatué, the people of Guarionex built a house next to the chapel in which we had left some images before which the catechumens might kneel and pray and find comfort. These catechumens were the mother, the brothers, and the relatives of the aforesaid Juan Mateo, the first Christian, whom another seven people had joined; and afterwards all those of his household became Christians, and they persisted in their good intention according to our faith. Thus it was that the whole family remained to guard the chapel and some fields I had tilled or had ordered tilled. And those people having

152. Ulloa: *Mauiatuè* and thus two more times, once at the beginning of the next chapter and again a few lines below that. When Ulloa mentions him in the next to the last paragraph of the text, he calls him *Mahuuiatiuire*. If we supply the missing letters in brackets, *Ma-[hu]-bia-t[i]-ue-[re]* and *Ma-hu-bia-ti-ui-re* are the same name. In the composition of this anthroponym, *Mabia ~ máhubia* could be the Arawak word *mabia* "honey." The ending *-tibere* has been conserved in popular Cuban speech in *guatíbere* "timid farmer" (Rodríguez Herrera, *Léxico mayor*, 1:70).
153. Here the text reads *Guariones*.

stayed behind as custodians of the chapel, on the second day after we had left to go to the aforesaid Mabiatué, six men went to the chapel, which the said catechumens, seven in number, had under their custody, and by order of Guarionex they told them to take those images that Fray Ramón[154] had left in the care of the catechumens, to destroy them, and break them because Fray Ramón and his companions had left and would not know who had done it. For the six servants of Guarionex who went there found the six boys who were in charge of the chapel, fearing what indeed happened thereafter. And the boys, thus indoctrinated, said they did not want them to come in. But they entered by force, and they took the images and carried them away.

CHAPTER XXVI

Concerning what happened to the images and the
miracle God worked to show his power

Having left the chapel, those men threw the images on the ground and covered them with earth and then urinated on them, saying: "Now your fruits will be good and great." This was because they buried them in a cultivated field, saying that the fruit of what had been planted there would be good; and all this as a vituperation.[155] When the boys who were guarding the chapel by order of the aforesaid catechumens saw this, they ran to their elders, who were in their fields, and they told them that the people of Guarionex had destroyed and mocked the images. When they found this out, they left what they were doing and ran shouting to inform Don Bartolomé Columbus, who had been entrusted with that government by the Admiral his brother, who had gone to Castile.[156] The former, as deputy of the Viceroy and Governor of the Islands, brought the wrongdoers to trial, and when the truth was known, he had them publicly burned. But with all this, Guarionex and his subjects did not put aside their evil intention of killing the Christians on the day designated for them to take them the tribute in gold they paid. But their plot was discovered, and thus they were taken prisoner on that same day they wanted to put their design into effect. And in spite of all this, they persisted in their perverse intention, and carrying it out, they killed four

154. In the text, unusually: *frate Romano.*
155. Not as vituperation, but as part of an agricultural rite in which they had the custom of burying a lithic representation of Yúcahu Bagua Maórocoti in their cultivations so that he might fertilize the sowing.
156. Columbus was absent from Hispaniola from March 1496 until August 1498.

men and Juan Mateo, a principal Christian,[157] and his brother Antón,[158] who had received the holy baptismal water. And they ran to the place where they had hidden the images and destroyed them. Some days later, the owner of that field went to dig up his *ajes* [yams],[159] which are certain roots like turnips, and others similar to radishes; and in the place where the images had been buried, two or three yams had grown as if they had put one across the other in the shape of a cross. It was not possible for anyone to find such a cross, and nevertheless it was found by the mother of Guarionex, the worst woman I have known in those parts, and she took it to be a great miracle, and she said to the commander of the fortress of Concepción: "This miracle has been wrought by God where the images were found. God knows why."

Let us now speak of how the first men who received holy baptism became Christians and what needs to be done so that they all might become Christians. And truly the island has a great need of people to punish the lords when they deserve it and to enlighten those peoples about the matters of the holy Catholic faith and to indoctrinate them in it because they cannot and they know not how to resist. And I can say it truly, for I have worn myself out in order to learn all this, and I am certain it will have been understood from what we have said up to now, and a word to the wise is sufficient.

The first Christians on the Island of Hispaniola, then, were those whom we have mentioned above, to wit, Guanabuariù,[160] in whose household there were seventeen people, all of whom became Christians

---

157. Ulloa: *principal scriuano,* and thus it has been translated as "escribano mayor" ("principal scribe") in the Madrid edition of 1932, 2:87, and as "chief clerk" in the Bourne version, *Columbus,* p. 30. The exalted missionary tone of the entire chapter leads one to think that this is a case of another mistaken reading: *escribano* (scribe) for what may perhaps have been the abbreviation for *cristiano* (Christian). In the context of this chapter, it seems logical to suppose that Pané would emphasize the fact that Juan Mateo was the "principal Christian" and makes little sense that he might be a "principal scribe."

158. Ulloa: *Antonio.* See note 142.

159. Ulloa: *agi* and thus two more times in this same paragraph. In some versions (that of Mexico City, 1947, for example), it has been translated as *ajíes* (chili peppers). It is, however, not *ajíes* but *ajes. Ajíes* are a variety of pepper. *Ajes* were a variety of the tubers also called *batatas, boniatos,* or *camotes* (yams). See Pedro Henríquez Ureña, "El enigma del aje," in his *Para la historia de los indigenismos* (Buenos Aires, 1938), pp. 59–86.

160. Ulloa: *Gianauuariù.* Cf. notes 138 and 141. One should note that in chapter XXV (notes 136 and 138), Pané calls the lord of the household *Guanáoboconel,* and there is a total of sixteen people in it. Here he calls him *Guanabuariù* (or perhaps *Guanaboría?*), and the total reaches seventeen people. The incongruencies may perhaps be due to carelessness in the translation.

simply by our teaching them there is a God, who made all things and created the heaven and the earth, without any other thing being discussed or taught to them because they were inclined to believe easily. But with the others there is need for force and ingenuity because we are not all made of the same stuff. Although those people made a good beginning and a better end, there will be others who will begin well and afterwards will laugh at what has been taught them; with them there is need for force and punishment.

The first who received holy baptism on the Island of Hispaniola was Juan Mateo, who was baptized on the day of the Evangelist Saint Matthew in the year of 1496,[161] and afterwards his whole household, in which there were many Christians. And the work would go forward if there were someone to indoctrinate them and teach them the holy Catholic faith and people to guide them. And if someone were to ask me why I believe this business to be so easy, I will say I have seen it in my own experience and especially in a principal *cacique* called Mahubiatíbire,[162] who has continued to be of good will for three years now, saying he wishes to be a Christian, and who wants to have but one wife, although they usually have two or three, and the principal men have ten, fifteen, and twenty.

This is what I have been able to find out and understand about the customs and rites of the Indians of Hispaniola by means of the diligence I have invested in the endeavor. I do not seek any spiritual or temporal advantage from it. Should it redound to his benefit and service, may it please Our Lord to grant me grace to be able to carry on; and if it is to be otherwise, may he take away my understanding.

End of the work of the humble friar Ramón Pané[163]

---

161. The day of the Evangelist Saint Matthew falls on September 21.
162. Here the text reads: *Mahuuiatiuire*. See note 152.
163. This colophon reads as follows: "Il fine dell'opera del pouero eremita Roman Pane." Thus, once again, the errors in the name and its accentuation as a paroxytone to which I have referred.

GROUP PRESENTATION #11

1. Considering the behique techniques, rituals, and ceremonies throughout the documentation presented by Friar Pane, does this documentation illustrate the old rivalry between civilization and nature? Which is preferred over the other by Pane and how would Christianity assist him in preferring one over the other? Was this "humble friar" ethnocentric?

2. According to Pane's attitude towards the behique, would you think Friar Pane would consider the behique more as the noble savage or as the wild man?

APPENDICES

[To the first European explorer of America himself we owe the first information we have about Taíno beliefs. Wishing to inform the Spanish
sovereigns about the nature of their new subjects and, perhaps, influ-
enced by the Renaissance currents rising in his native Italy and spreading
throughout Europe, Columbus displayed from the first moment of his
arrival a lively curiosity about the rites and customs of the inhabitants of
the islands where he had just landed. Products of that curiosity are the
brief notes he wrote in his *Diario del primer viaje* (1492–1493), the summary he made of those notes in a paragraph of a letter he sent to Luis
de Santángel announcing the discovery of the New World (1493), and a
passage relating what he managed to gather during the period he resided
in Hispaniola on the second voyage (1493–1496).

Columbus's reports are scant, and they give us at times a somewhat
blurry image, as if his lack of perspective left them a bit out of focus. But
those hints, in spite of their deficiencies, supply a few details not given
in the other existing sources about Taíno myths and ceremonies. Their
value as direct testimony is undeniable, of course, and I have thought
it thus useful to gather in one place the pertinent data from the three
documents.

With regard to the sources of the texts, the original *Diario del primer
viaje* has been lost; there remains only the extract made by Father Las
Casas. I have excerpted the *Diario* passages he quotes from the facsimile
edition of Las Casas's manuscript prepared by Carlos Sanz (Madrid,
1962). The second piece is taken from the *Carta de Colón anunciando el
descubrimiento del Nuevo Mundo, 15 de febrero–14 de marzo. Reproducción
del texto original español, impreso en Barcelona, Pedro Posa, 1493* (Madrid,
1956). The passage quoted by Fernando in his biography of his father
appears in chapter 62. That work is known only in the Italian version

translated by Alfonso de Ulloa and published in Venice in 1571. I have prepared a new Spanish translation of the passage, attending more to its accuracy than to its literary style.]

DIARY OF THE FIRST VOYAGE

[On the northeast coast of Cuba]
Monday 29 October
They found many statues of female figures and many head-shaped masks, very well carved. I do not know if they keep these for their beauty or if they worship them.

Thursday 1 November
These people, the Admiral says, are of the same type and customs as those we have found before; they have no religion I know of, for until now I have not seen those I have brought with me make any prayer, except they say the Salve and the Ave Maria, with their hands pointed toward heaven as they are taught, and they make the sign of the cross.

Monday 12 November
Because I saw it for myself and I know—says the Admiral—these people have no religion at all, nor are they idolaters; rather they are very gentle . . . and ingenuous, and they know there is a God in heaven, and they are convinced that we have come from heaven, and they are very quick with any prayer we teach them to say, and they make the sign of the cross.

Thursday 29 November
In one house the sailors also found a man's skull inside a little basket hanging from a post in the house, and in another village they found another one just like it. The Admiral believed it must have belonged to some important members of one lineage because those houses were of such a kind that many people live in each one, and they must be related, descendents of the same ancestor.

[On the northwest coast of Hispaniola]
Saturday 22 December
The lord of that region, who had a place near there, sent him a great canoe full of people, and in it he sent one of his leading retainers to beg the Admiral to go with the ships to his country and he would give him everything he had. He sent him with the ambassador a belt that had, in

place of a pouch, a mask that had two large ears, the tongue, and the nose made of hammered gold.

Wednesday 26 December
They brought the Admiral a large mask that had large pieces of gold in the ears and eyes and other parts, which he presented him along with other pieces of gold jewelry.

LETTER FROM COLUMBUS ANNOUNCING THE
DISCOVERY OF THE NEW WORLD

[15 February–14 March 1493]
And besides this, they will become Christians, for they are inclined to the love and service of Your Majesties and of the entire Castillian nation, and they try to help and share with us the things they have in abundance that we need. And they knew no religion or idolatry, except they all believe that the power and the good is in heaven. And they believed very strongly that I came, with these ships and people, from heaven, and with due respect they receive me everywhere after they have lost their fear. And this is not because they are ignorant; rather they are of keen wit, and they are men who sail all those seas, for the good account they give of everything is a marvel, except that they never saw people in clothes or such ships. And after I reached the Indies, on the first island I found, I took some of them by force so that they might advise and inform me what was in that region. And thus it was that later they understood us and we them, whether in words or by signs, and they have learned a great deal. Nowadays those I am carrying with me always maintain that I come from heaven, no matter how much conversation they have had with me. And these were the first to declare it wherever I went, and the others would go running from house to house and to nearby villages shouting, "Come to see the people from heaven." And after they felt secure with us, all of them came, both men and women, for not even the elderly or the young would stay behind, and all of them would bring something to eat and to drink, which they offered with marvelous love.

THE ADMIRAL'S WORDS [CA. 1496]

I have not succeeded in discerning among them either idolatry or other sect, although all their kings, and there are many of them on Hispaniola as well as on the other islands and on the mainland, have a house for each one of them, separate from the population, in which there is nothing other than images of wood, carved in relief, that they call zemis, nor in that house is work done for any other purpose or service than for these zemis, with a certain ceremony and prayer, which they go there to make, as we go to church. In this house they have a well-carved table, round in shape, like a chopping block, on which there are some powders they put on the head of the aforesaid zemis, making a certain ceremony; afterwards they inhale this powder with a forked tube they put into the nose. None of us understands the words they say. With the said powder they go into a frenzy, becoming as if drunken. They give a name to the said statue, which I believe must be their father's, their grandfather's, or both because they have more than one, and some have more than ten, all in memory as I have already said of some of their ancestors. I have indeed heard them praise one more than another, and I have seen them show more devotion and make more reverence to one than another, as we do in processions when it is necessary. And the *caciques* and their people take pride in having better zemis than others do. And when they go to these zemis and enter the house where they are kept, they avoid the Christians and do not let them enter: on the contrary, if they suspect the Christians are approaching, they take the zemi or zemis and hide them in the forest for fear that the Christians might take them away. And, what is more laughable, they have among themselves the custom of stealing the zemis from each other. And it happened on one occasion that they were wary of us, and the Christians entered with them into the said house, and suddenly the zemi shouted loudly and spoke in their language. From this it was discovered that they were made with artifice; they were hollow and in the lower part was inserted a horn or trumpet that came out on the back side of the house and was covered with leaves and branches, where a person stood who would pronounce what the *cacique* wanted him to say, as much as can be said through a trumpet. Therefore, our people, suspecting what that could be, kicked the zemi and found it to be as I have related. Seeing that our people had discovered the business, the *cacique* begged them with a fervent plea not to say anything to the Indians, his subjects or others, because he held them all in obedience with that trick. From this we can say there may have been some taint of idolatry, at least in those who do not know the *caciques'* secret and deceit, for they believe the zemi is the one who speaks, and all of them generally are deceived, and only the *cacique* knows and conceals the false credulity he uses to extract from his people all the tributes he wants. Likewise, most of the *caciques* have three stones that they and their people hold in great devotion. One they say is good for the grains and vegetables they have sown, the other for women to give birth without pain, and the third for water and sun when they have need of them. I sent Your Highness three of these stones with Antonio de Torres, and I will take another three with me. Also, when these Indians die, they arrange their funeral rites in various ways. And this is the manner in which they bury the *caciques:* they open the *cacique* and dry him by the fire, so he will thus be preserved whole. From others they take only the head. Others they bury in a cave and put bread and a gourd of water on their heads. Others they burn in the house where they die, and when they see them in their final extremity, they do not let them end their life, but rather they strangle them, and this is done with the *caciques.* Others they throw out of the house, and others they put in a hammock, which is their net bed, and they put water and bread next to their heads, and they leave them alone, not seeing them again. Also others who are gravely ill they take to the *cacique,* and he tells them if they ought to be strangled or not, and they do what he orders. I have endeavored greatly to find out what they believe and if they know where they go after death, especially from Caonabó, who was the principal king of Hispaniola, a man advanced in years and of great knowledge and very keen understanding. And he and the others answered that they go to a certain valley, which each principal *cacique* believes is located in his country; they affirm they find their parents and all their ancestors there, and they eat and have women and give themselves to pleasures and comforts. This is described in greater detail in the following document, an account from a certain Fray Ramón, who knew their language, whom I commissioned to collect information on their rites and antiquities. Although, the fables are so abundant one cannot gather any fruit except that each one of them has a certain natural respect for the future and believes in the immortality of our souls.

[Although he never set foot in the New World, Peter Martyr—as Pietro Martire d'Anghiera has traditionally been known in the English-speaking world—managed to gather more information about the Indies than almost any of his contemporaries. A man with a facile pen and an insatiable curiosity, he missed no opportunity to seize upon and convey—in a Latin that is at once both nimble and expressive—to his delighted correspondents the latest news arriving from America. His letters, which soon increased in volume and transcendence, became the basis of his *De Orbe Novo Decades*, a work of inestimable value for the study of this period.

Thanks to his friendship with Columbus, Peter Martyr was afforded the opportunity to see Pané's manuscript. So moved was he by the novelty of the information contained in this account that he summarized those portions he considered of greatest interest in a letter to Cardinal Ludovico of Aragón. From that letter, which later became part of the ninth chapter of the first *Decade*, we cite below the passage that touches upon our subject.

The new Spanish translation (of which this English text is a translation) is based on the 1587 edition, carefully edited by the English scholar Richard Hakluyt: *De Orbe Novo Petri Martyris Anglerii . . . Parisiis, apud Gvillelmvm Avvary*, 1587. For greater certainty, the text established by Hakluyt has been compared, particularly with regard to Taíno words, with the edition of the *De Orbe Novo Decades*, Alcalá de Henares, 1516, published under the supervision and care of Antonio de Nebrija. Two earlier Spanish translations have also been taken into account: the version by Joaquín Torres de Asensio in his *Fuentes históricas sobre Colón y América*, 2d ed., Madrid, Imprenta de la S.E. de San Francisco de Sales, 1829; *Décadas del Nuevo Mundo, vertidas del Latín a lengua castellana . . .* (Buenos Aires, Editorial Bajel, 1944), and the translation by

Agustín Millares Carlo (Mexico City, José Porrúa e hijos, 1964–1965). Given the testimonial purpose of our version, we have avoided Antillean expressions not used by Anghiera (hence, *"régulos"* [kinglets] has been used instead of *"caciques"*), and we have made an effort to reproduce the Taíno terms just as they appear in the text, but adapting them to Spanish norms of spelling (for example, *"Macocael"* instead of *"Machochael"*). Given the length of the passage, it has been divided into paragraphs.]

A certain brother Ramón, a dedicated friar who lived for a long time among the island kinglets by Columbus's order, so that he might indoctrinate them in Christian teachings, wrote a little book in Spanish about the rites of the island dwellers. From his writings I have proposed to collect these few details, omitting other more trivial items. Here you have them:

It is well known that nocturnal spirits appear to the islanders so as to lure them into vain errors, and this is known from the idols they worship in public. For they make seated images of stuffed woven cloth that look like the nocturnal specters our painters paint on the walls. Because you yourself have seen four of those images, which I ordered sent to you, you can personally show his Highness the King, your uncle, better than I can describe them, how they are like the painted specters.

The indigenous people call these images zemis; the smallest, which represent little devils, they tie to their foreheads when they go to fight with their enemies. That is why they are tied with the cords you saw. They think they receive from these the rain when it is needed and the sun if they need that, for they believe the zemis are messengers from Him who they confess is one, infinite, omnipotent, and invisible. Every kinglet has his zemi whom he worships. His ancestors gave to the Everlasting God in heaven these two names: Iocaúna, Guamaónocon. They say the same god has a mother, called by these five names, to wit: Attabeira, Mamona, Guacarapita, Iiella, Guimazoa.

Note what they childishly say about the origin of man in their land: there is a region on the island called Caunaná, where it is said humankind emerged from two caves in a certain mountain: most of the men emerged from the widest mouth of the cavern; a smaller number, from the narrowest. The rock in which the caves are found is called Cauta; the larger cave, Cazibaxagua; the smaller Amaiauna.

Their naive story relates that before men were allowed to emerge from there, the mouths of the cavern were guarded every night by a man called Mácocael. This Mácocael went too far away from the cave, wanting to look around, and was surprised by the sun, whose presence had not been granted him to tolerate in the slightest, and they say he was changed into stone. They speak also of many others who had gone away from the cave at night intending to fish and had gone so far away that they could not return before the sun came out, which it was not licit for them to gaze upon, and they were changed into myrobalan trees, which that land produces spontaneously in abundance.

They say likewise that Vaguoniona, a principal man, had sent a certain man to leave the cave to fish, unbeknownst to his relatives, and he was changed into a nightingale for the same reason that the sun had come out before he returned. They affirm that every year, at the season when he became a little bird, he laments his fate at night in his song and implores his lord Vaguoniona for aid. They think the nightingale sings at night for this reason.

In truth, missing his relative whom he dearly loved, Vaguoniona abandoned the men in the cave and took out only the women with the babies they were suckling. They say that on his journey he left the women on one of the islands, which they call Matininó, and he took the children with him. As these poor little ones, distressed by hunger, were crying "toa, toa"—that is, "mama, mama"—on the shore of a certain river, they were changed into frogs they say, and since then frogs speak with that voice in springtime. Thus they tell the obscure tale that only males without females remained in those caverns from which men spread throughout Hispaniola.

They tell likewise that the same Vaguoniona, who was wandering about in various places and nevertheless, by special grace, was never transformed like the others, went down toward a beautiful woman he saw in the depth of the sea, and from her he received some little marble stones that they call *cibas* and certain little gilded brass laminas that they call *guanines*. The kings hold these necklaces sacred even today.

Of those men who remained in the caves without women, as we have said, they tell that when they went out at night to bathe in the pools of rain water, they saw from afar certain animals like women who were climbing in the myrobalan trees, like squadrons of ants: they ran toward those female-looking animals; they caught them, and like eels they slipped from their hands.

Then they made a decision. On the advice of the elders, they looked for the mangy and leprous men who lived among them and who had rough and callused hands with which they could more easily capture and hold the creatures. They call these men *caracaracoles*. They went out to hunt the creatures, and of the many they caught, they held on to only four: they tried to use them like women, but they discovered they lacked the female sex.

Having joined the elders once again, they consulted them about what they should do. And they decided to send a search for the carpenter bird, who with his sharp beak could make a hole between the thighs while the same callused *caracaracoles* men held the women's legs open. As soon as they brought the carpenter bird, he opened the women's sex; in this very lovely way, the island had the women it desired: thus they procreated their descendents. Come, stop being astounded by what truthful Greece narrated in so many volumes about the dwarves, like their having been engendered by ants. These and many other similar things the wisest men read aloud as a sacred matter from their tribunals and platforms and convince the simple and amazed multitude.

The business of the origin of the sea is more serious. Regarding this they say there was in ancient times on the island a powerful man called Iaia. When his only son died, he put him into a squash instead of into a sepulcher. A few months later, impatient because of his son's death, Iaia went to see the squash again; and when he had opened it, enormous whales and great cetaceans came out, whereby he informed certain neighbors that the sea was enclosed in that squash. Attracted by that rumor, four young brothers, born from the same birth in which their mother died, went to the squash in the hope of getting fish and took it in their hands. Iaia, who frequently returned to see his son's bones enclosed there, was then arriving, and the young men were frightened. Caught in the sacrilege and under suspicion of theft, because they respected Iaia, they dropped the squash so as to flee more quickly, and because of the excess weight, it broke. The sea spilled out through the cracks, the valleys filled up; that vast surface of that dry world of the island came under water, and the only part spared from that flood, because of their altitude, were the mountains that form the islands we can see now.

Here you have, illustrious prince, the origin of the sea, worthy of the greatest renown: and don't believe they have any lack of esteem for whomever has learned to recite these matters. They say also that these brothers, for fear of Iaia, wandered in various places for so long that they nearly starved to death because they did not dare to stop anywhere. And because hunger was afflicting them then so cruelly, they began to knock at the home of a baker and beg for *cazabe*, that is to say, bread; but they tell that the baker spat so violently at the first one who entered that from the blow of the spit a tumor grew on him, very swollen, and he nearly died; but taking a sharp rock on the advice of his brothers, he opened it, and they tell that from the ulcer a woman was born, whom all the brothers used mutually, and upon her they engendered sons and daughters.

Listen to another more agreeable thing, illustrious prince. There exists a cavern called Iouanaboina in the territory of a certain little king called Maquinnec, which they revere and venerate more piously than the Greeks did Corinth or Cirra and Nisa in ancient times, and they have it adorned with a thousand kinds of paintings, and at the entrance of this cavern they have two sculpted zemis, one of whom they call Bintaitel and the other Marohu. When they were asked why they had such pious veneration for the cavern, they answered seriously and sensibly because from there emerged the sun and the moon that were to give light to the world. They make pilgrimages to visit the caverns as we do to Rome and the Vatican, head of our religion, or to Compostela and Jerusalem, sepulchre of the Lord.

They are also immersed in another sort of superstition. They think the dead wander at night and eat the fruit *guannaba*, unknown to us and like the quince, and they get into bed among the living, and they deceive women, for when they take the shape of a man, it appears they wish to cohabit, but when they reach the act, they disappear. And if anyone, noticing anything strange in the bed, suspects that perhaps a dead person is lying with her, they tell that she makes certain by touching its stomach, for they say the dead can acquire every human part except the navel; if by the navel, then, she recognizes that it is a dead person, when she touches it, it vanishes at once. They believe the dead often come out at night to meet the living, primarily on the roads and public ways, and if a traveler stands bravely in front of it, the phantom dissolves; but if in effect he is afraid, it terrorizes him so that, having at him, frequently from that fear many fall ill and end up dimwitted.

When our people asked the islanders from where they had got those vain and harmful rites, they answer that they have inherited them from their ancestors; they say those things have been transmitted in that way in songs from time immemorial, and it is not licit to teach them to anyone other than the sons of the lords. They learn them by heart because they have never had writing, and singing them to the people on holidays, they recite them as sacred solemnities. They have a single instrument made of wood, concave, resonant, which is beaten like a drum.

Their soothsayers, whom they call *boítios*, inculcate these superstitions in them; the soothsayers are also physicians who commit a thousand deceptions on the poor ignorant people. These soothsayers make the people believe; indeed, they enjoy great authority among them, for the zemis themselves speak to them and predict future matters to them. And if any sick man gets well, they persuade him that he has achieved this by the grace of the zemi.

The *boítios* are obliged to fast and to purge themselves when they take charge of the care of some principal man, and they eat an intoxicating herb, which when they inhale it in powder makes them as mad as the Maenads, and they are heard to say that they have heard many things from the zemis. When they visit a sick man, they carry a bone, a little stone, or a little piece of meat in their mouths, and they send everyone out of the room except one or two whom the patient himself has chosen.

Twisting his face, lips, and nose the *boítio* takes three or four turns around the person; with ugly gestures he blows on his forehead, temple, and neck, inhaling the breath of the sick man; after he has done this, he says he has extracted the sickness from the patient's veins. Then rubbing the sick man on his shoulders, thighs, and legs, he pulls his intertwined hands away from the man's feet, and with his hands thus together, he runs toward the door, which is open, and opening up his hands, he shakes them as if he were throwing out the evil, and he persuades him that he has taken his illness away, and soon the sick man will recover. Then, approaching him from behind, he takes the little piece of meat out of his mouth like a prestidigitator and shouts at the sick man, say-ing: "Look what you have eaten in excess: now you will get well because I have taken it away from you." But if he wants to deceive the sick man even more seriously, he persuades him that his zemi is angry because either he did not build it a house, or he did not render it the appropri-ate religious ceremony, or he did not dedicate a property to it. If the sick man should die, his relatives meet and by sorcery make the dead man declare if he died by the hand of fate or because of the negligence of the *boítio* because he did not fast altogether or because he did not give the sick man the appropriate medicine. If he died by the physician's fault, they take revenge on him.

If the women get any of the little stones or bones that some *boítio* is thought to have carried in his mouth, they keep them reverently wrapped in little cloths, for they believe they can be of great service in childbirth, and the women have those little stones instead of zemis.

The zemis that various islanders worship are different. Some, advised by nocturnal shadows among the trees, make them of wood. Others, if they found answers among the rocks, make them of stone. Those that are found among the *ajes*—that is to say, the kind of food of which we spoke before—are worshiped on the roots of *ajes*. They say the concern of these zemis is for that bread to be made. As the ancients thought that the dryads, hamadryades, satyrs, fauns, and nereids guarded the foun-tains, forests, and the sea, and they assigned a god to each thing so that each kind would be protected by its deity, thus these islanders think that their zemis, invoked, listen to their wishes. And thus, when the king-lets consult the zemis about issues of war, about harvests, about health, they enter the house dedicated to the zemi and there inhale through their nostrils the *cohoba*, for thus they call the intoxicating herb; with which *cohoba* the *boítios* also suddenly begin to rave, and at once they say they begin to see that the house is moving, turning things upside down, and that men are walking backwards. Such is the efficacy of that ground powder of the *cohoba* that it immediately takes the sense away from him who takes it.

Scarcely does the madness leave him when he puts his head down, grasping his legs with his arms, and staying stupified awhile in this state, he lifts his head like a somnambulent, and raising his eyes to heaven, first he babbles certain confused things, and then the nobles of his court, who surround him (for no plebeian is admitted to these sacred acts), give him thanks aloud for having returned to them after his colloquy with the zemis, and they ask him what he has seen. And opening his mouth, he raves that the zemi has counseled him during that time, and as if possessed by frenzy, he explains to them that the zemi has predicted to him either victory or ruin if they go to battle with the enemy, hunger or abundance, plague or health, and whatever comes to his mind. Come, illustrious prince, after this, how are you to be amazed at the spirit of Apollo who brandishes his words with immense fury? And you thought that superstitious antiquity had ended!

Because we have related so many general things about the zemis, it seems to me that I ought not pass over in silence what is told in particular of one of them. They say that a certain *cacique* Guamareto had a zemi called Corocoto. They tell about him that many times he came down from the highest part of the house where Guamareto kept him tied, breaking his bonds, sometimes wanting to cohabit, sometimes to eat, sometimes to hide, and that at times he was hidden several days, angry that the *cacique* Guamareto had failed in his cult and ceremonies.

They tell that in Guamareto's court sometimes children have been born who have two crowns, and they are of the opinion that they are sons of the zemi Corocoto. They tell likewise that Guamareto was beaten in battle by his enemies, and his court and royal house were completely devastated by blood and fire, but that when they set the house on fire, Corocoto freed himself from his bonds and leaped a stadium's distance away, where afterwards they found him.

There is another zemi called Epileguanita, four-legged and made of wood, who many times, according to what they say, escaped to the forest from the place in which he was worshiped. As often as they would discover he had escaped, they would carefully go in a procession to look for him, with pious prayers, and when they found him, they would carry him reverently on their shoulders to the sanctuary dedicated to him. But they complained that when the Christians went to the island, he fled, and they have never again found him anywhere; and taking it as an evil omen, they weep for the ruin of their fatherland. These things have been learned from the mouths of the elders.

They worshiped another zemi of stone, of female sex, which two men attended as ministers. One of these men, by order of the female, filled the office of proclaimer to the rest of the zemis who, by her command, lent their assistance in conjuring the winds, the rains, and the clouds; they say the other man, by her order, gathered in the valleys the waters that ran from the high mountains so that from there, pouring out with torrential force, they might devastate the fields if the natives had not rendered to her image the promised fitting honors.

Listen, finally, illustrious prince, to another thing worthy of memory with which the work may be finished. Our people found among the islanders the very sad story that there were in other times two kinglets, one of whom was the progenitor of Guarionex, whom we have already mentioned many times. The two abstained from eating and drinking for a five-day period so that the zemis would reveal to them something of future matters. Having made themselves agreeable to the zemis with that fast, they recounted that the zemis answered them that not many years would go by before a people covered with clothes would reach that island, and they would end all those rites and ceremonies of the island and would kill all their children or deprive them of freedom. Conjecturing that this referred to the cannibals, the youths resolved to save themselves by flight when they saw them approaching, and never again did they enter into combat with them. But when truly they saw the Spaniards who invaded their island, consulting among themselves about this matter, they resolved that they were that people of the prophecy. And they were not mistaken; they are all now subject to the Christians, and all those who resisted are dead: not even a memory is now left of the zemis, who have been transported to Spain so that we might be acquainted with their mockery and the devils' deceptions: you have seen many of them, illustrious prince, through my diligence. ·

I pass over many things because you have warned me that tomorrow without fail you will return to the fatherland to rejoin the queen, your elder aunt, whom you accompanied here by order of your uncle King Federico. You [are] ready to travel, and I weary, so have a good time and remember your Martire, whom you have obliged, in the name of your uncle Federico, to select these few bits of news from among a wealth of them.

APPENDIX C

FRAY BARTOLOMÉ DE LAS CASAS

[Of all the chroniclers, Fray Bartolomé de Las Casas was without a doubt the most well informed about the early inhabitants of the Antilles. His long residence on the islands and his fervent effort to win humanitarian treatment of the natives led him to familiarize himself with the habits and customs of his flock. He was a tireless writer as well, and he left a very copious body of work. Of his principal books, the *Breve historia de la destrucción de las Indias* is a compendium of the arguments he wielded in his outraged indictment of the excesses he witnessed. The extensive *Historia de las Indias,* completed in the serenity of a productive old age, is the most complete and authoritative version of the events that took place in America during his lifetime. The *Apologética historia de las Indias,* perhaps the most complex and well documented of the three, is in fact the *summa theologica* in the defense of the dignity of the Indian. In his search for documentary sources for this work, he handled Pané's manuscript and summarized portions of it in chapters 120, 166, and 167. This part of the text, however, constitutes something more than a simple summary. At times he corrects Pané's testimony, and at times he amplifies it with his own firsthand information.

The text that here follows is based directly on the holographic manuscript preserved in the Royal Academy of History (Muñoz Collection A-73). In accordance with the norms followed in the transcription of the other documents appearing here, the spelling and accentuation have been modernized, and the text has been divided into paragraphs. This reading has also been compared with the editions produced by Manuel Serrano y Sanz (Madrid, 1909) and by Juan Pérez de Tudela y Bueso (Madrid, 1958).]

Concerning the idols worshiped by the Indians of the Island of Hispaniola
Because I have already discussed very thoroughly the gods of the ancient gentiles of so many centuries past, whereby their very gross blindness and deception have been well demonstrated, it is now time henceforward to consider the gods of these our Indian peoples. Either they received and inherited these gods from those ancient idolators, as is likely, at least in great part, or they invented them and added to them. Thus we can compare them in this regard, as will be done with other topics. It is appropriate to speak first of the inhabitants of this Island of Hispaniola and of the other islands, for they were discovered before any others; we shall proceed in the order which we established at the outset.

To begin, one should know that the peoples of this Hispaniola and the Island of Cuba and that which we call San Juan and that of Jamaica and all the islands of the Bahamas and generally all the rest that are almost in a row, moving from West to East for more than five hundred maritime leagues, from close to the Mainland called Florida up to the tip of the peninsula of Paria [Venezuela] on the Mainland and also along the sea coast, the peoples of the Mainland along that shore of the Gulf of Paria, and all that area from there down as far as Veragua [the coast of Panama], almost all those peoples had one kind of religion, and little or almost none at that, although they had some sort of idolatry. They did not have temples in many places, and those they had were of little merit because they were no more than straw houses like the other ordinary houses, set somewhat apart; they had but a few idols, and these were meant to be worshiped not because they were gods, but rather because of the fantasies that certain priests invested in them, and the devil invested in the priests, to the effect that they could do them some good, like give them children and send them water and other such useful things. They held only infrequent visible or audible ceremonies, and those were practiced by those priests who, deceived and appointed by the devil as his ministers, practiced them with certain cunning pretenses. Their religion seems primarily to have abided in the idea or respect of a god, and there they held their worship, although some errors intruded because they lacked doctrine and grace, and the devil and his ministers put obstacles before them and worked persuasions upon them.

The people of this Island of Hispaniola had a certain faith in and knowledge of a one and true God, who was immortal and invisible, for none can see him, who had no beginning, whose dwelling place and residence is heaven, and they called him Yócahu Vagua Maórocoti. I do not know what they meant by this name because when I could indeed have found it out, I did not think to inquire.

Into this true and catholic knowledge of the true God these errors intruded, to wit: that God had a mother, whose name was Atabex, and a brother Guaca and other relatives in like fashion. They must have been like people without a guide on the road of the truth; rather, there was one who would lead them astray, clouding the light of their natural reason that could have guided them.

According to what the Admiral Don Christopher Columbus wrote in a letter to the Sovereigns, they had certain statues of wood where they placed the bones of their fathers (and they had to be those of kings and lords), and they called these statues by the name of the person whose bones were therein enclosed. They tell that a man would get inside them because they were hollow and there speak what the king or lord told him to say to the commoners.

And it happened that when two Spaniards entered the house where one of those statues was placed, the statue appeared to give a shout and speak certain words, but because Spaniards are not easily astounded by shouting sticks, one of them approached and kicked the statue, and it fell on its side, and thus he discovered the secret of what was inside. The secret was that on one side of the house there must have been a hole or a certain space in the corner, covered with branches, where the person who was speaking was concealed, and he had a trumpet or blowpipe that he inserted through the hollow of the statue, and when he spoke into it, the statue appeared to be speaking. The Admiral says more: that he had endeavored to find out if the peoples of this island had any religion that smacked of clear idolatry, and he had not been able to ascertain it; for that reason, he had sent a Catalan who had taken a friar's habit, and they called him Fray Ramón, a simple man of good intention who knew something of the language of the Indians, that he might investigate and set down in writing all that might further be learned about the rites and religion and antiquities of the peoples of this island.

This Fray Ramón found out what he could, insofar as he understood the languages, for there were three spoken on this island; he knew only one, however, that of a small province that we said above was called Lower Macorix, and he knew that language only imperfectly. Of the universal language he knew very little, like the rest of the Spaniards, although more than the others because no one—neither clergyman, friar, nor layman—knew any of them perfectly except for a sailor from Palos or from Moguer who was called Cristóbal Rodríguez, the interpreter, and I do not believe the latter altogether fathomed the one he knew, which was the general one, although no one knew it except him. And this business of no one's knowing the languages of this island was not because they were very difficult to learn, but rather because in those days no man either of the church or the laity took any care, great or small, to impart doctrine or knowledge of God to these people; instead, they all merely made use of them, wherefore they learned no more words in the languages than "give the bread here," "go to the mines," "take out gold," and such words as were necessary for the service of the Spaniards and the execution of their desires. Only this Fray Ramón, who came to this island at the beginning with the Admiral, seems to have had some zeal and goodwill, which he put into effect, for imparting a knowledge of God to these Indians. As a simple man, however, he did not know how to do it; rather, his efforts amounted to nothing more than to say the Ave María and Pater Noster to the Indians, and some words about there being a God in heaven who was the creator of things, according to what he was able to teach them with abundant flaws and in a muddled way. There were also on this island two friars of St. Francis, laymen, although good men, whom I met as I had Fray Ramón; they had good zeal, but they also lacked a good knowledge of the languages. These men were foreigners, either from Picardy or Burgundy; one was called Fray Juan el Bermejo or Borgoñón, and the other Fray Juan de Tisim.

The Admiral ordered this Fray Ramón to leave that province of Lower Macorix because their language, the one Fray Ramón knew, extended for only a small area and to go to the Vega and dominion of the king Guarionex, where he could gather more fruit because there were many more people there and their language was universal throughout the entire island. He did so and stayed no more than two years and did all he could there in accordance with his limited faculties; one of the two aforesaid Franciscan clergymen went with him.

Returning to the subject of the religion of the people of this island, what this Fray Ramón succeeded in learning was that they had some idols or good luck statues, and these were generally called *çemí*, the final syllable long and stressed. They believed these zemis gave them water and wind and sun when they had need of them, and likewise children and other things they wanted to have. Some of these were made of wood and others of stone. Fray Ramón relates that the ones of wood were made in this way: when an Indian was going along the road and saw some tree moving with the wind more than the others, of which the Indian was afraid, he would approach it and ask: "Who are you?" And the tree would answer: "Summon me here a *behique*, and he will tell you who I am." A *behique* was a priest or prophet or sorceror about whom more will be said below. When the *behique* arrived, he would approach the tree and, seated next to it, hold a certain ceremony; then he would stand and recite to it the dignities and titles of the principal lords of the island, asking it: "What are you doing here? What do you want of me? Why did you have me summoned? Tell me if you want me to cut you down, if you want to come with me, and how you want me to carry you because I will prepare a house and cultivated fields for you." In response, the tree then told him what he wanted and that he should cut it down, and told him the manner in which he was to prepare the house and land and the ceremonies he was to hold for it throughout the year. He would cut the tree and make from it a statue or idol, an ugly figure because ordinarily they fashion the faces with the expression of old scolding monkeys; he prepared the house and land for it, and each year he would hold certain ceremonies for it, to which he had recourse as to an oracle, asking and finding out from it future matters of good and evil, which afterwards he would preach to the common people.

All that has been said, about the tree's speaking and asking for the things it asked of the people, and of its ordering them to cut it down and make the said statue or image from it, all this is possible for the devil to accomplish with God's permission, and it may have been altogether true that he had such cunning and tricks to induce those simple people to his cult and idolatry, as appears to be borne out by the many things that have been well explained above. And in order to achieve his end, the first thing the devil attempts is to constitute ministers, deceiving those people he finds who are most disposed and inclined to the business, given to bad habits, and malicious. Among the gentiles and nations who are ignorant of and live without knowledge of the true God, the priests were always and are the ones to whom he first shows himself, and makes some particular gifts, and reveals or gives notice of some necessary truths so that they may be believed because with these priests he deceives all the rest. Thus did he do on this and the other islands with these very simple people, where the idolatry was not very widespread or very open and outrageous, and perhaps he had begun to deceive them only a few years earlier because his corruption of the whole human lineage with blindness to divine matters was not accomplished suddenly, but rather little by little, darkening their natural light that reveals and inclines men to search for the true God. And God, just and good, does not withdraw his grace from men at once; first he waits for them to be unworthy of it because of their sins, in accordance with what was explained above in detail. Thus it is that the devil must first convert his ministers and introduce them into the office and ministry of his priests; and it must have been sufficient industry on his part to get inside a tree and speak the aforesaid words and others for his purpose and to have a thousand other tricks and cunning in order to deceive some men first who he knew could help him in his evil deeds.

Indeed, these priests, who are called *behiques* in the language of these islands and who were their theologians, prophets, and soothsayers, practiced some deceptions upon these people, primarily when they acted as physicians, in accordance with what the devil, from the domain allowed to him, dictated to them what they were to say or do. They led the people to believe they spoke with those statues and that the statues revealed their secrets to them, and they find out from those secrets everything they want to know. And it must have been so because the devil surely spoke in those statues. The statues, however, were neither very many nor very serious, as we shall see if we put aside all the business with which the devil surrounded them so as to lead the people, as best he could, to the superstitions, branches, and circumstances of idolatry, which is what he is always up to and which, however small it may be, is evil and a large deception.

They had other idols or images of stone that those priests and physicians made the people believe they took out of the bodies of those who were sick, and these stones were of three kinds. I never saw their form, but they held each one to have its own power: one had the power to favor their sown lands; the second, so that women would have good fortune in childbirth; the power of the third was that they would have water and good rains when they had need of them. Thus they must have been like the gods of the ancients, each one of whom had the responsibility of presiding in his domain, although these peoples sensed this more crudely and simply than the ancients. The kings and lords boasted—and in this the other people must have followed them—about their zemis or gods and considered them more glorious, saying that they had better zemis than the other peoples and lords, and they endeavored to steal them from each other; and although they took great care in guarding these statues or idols, or whatever they may have been, from other Indians from other kingdoms and dominions, they took incomparably greater care in guarding and concealing them from the Spaniards, and when they suspected their approach, they would take them and hide them in the mountains. The ceremonies or sacrifices the *bohiques* or priests made to these statues, before they would ask them what they wanted to know, will be explained below.*

*The manuscript continues with the following testament:
"They went around in this manner. . . . [In the manuscript, folio 397 is cut. In the margin is written: Here is to be included in its entirety the following chapter, which begins:

Concerning the religion professed by the Indians of the Island of Hispaniola
Blessed be the Lord who has saved me from such a deep sea of sacrifices
like those gentiles, who so often were ignorant of the true sacrifice and
sailed blindly; although I have said a great deal about them, I could say
a great deal more. Henceforth, in accordance with the order we have set,

---

"Having related that which," etc.] completely hollow like a flute, two-thirds of the way
down it is separated into two tubes, in the way we separate the two first fingers after the
thumb. They placed those two tubes into both nostrils and the end of the flute, so to
speak, in the powder on the dish, and they inhaled; as they inhaled, they took in through
their nostrils the dose of powder they had decided to consume. When they had consumed
it, they immediately went out of their minds, and they ended up intoxicated, as if they
had drunk a great deal of strong wine. Those powders and these acts were called *cohoba*,
the middle syllable long in their language. They spoke in gibberish, confusedly, I know
not what, and then they were worthy of the colloquy with the statues or, more properly,
with the enemy of human nature who dwelled in them, and in this way the secrets were
revealed to them, and they prophesied. They heard and learned in this way if some good,
adversity, or harm was to come to them. This was when the priest merely made ready to
speak and for the statue to speak to him. But when all the leaders of the people gathered to
make *cohoba*, persuaded by the *behiques* or ordered by the lords, then it was amazing to see
them. In order to hold their councils or to decide difficult matters, such as if they ought to
make war or to undertake important matters, their custom was to make their *cohoba* and to
intoxicate themselves in that way. This manner of consultation, very full of wine and inebriated, was not original with these people because as it was . . . [gap in the manuscript]
I am a servant of God. And this man was called Juan, and in this manner and speaking
these words another man died called Antón, who was his brother. And thus Fray Ramón
says these men were martyrs, about which no Christian can harbor any doubt if they were
killed for their faith or for refusing to relinquish their faith or for some other virtue. But
they did not kill them for that reason because no Indian ever did such a thing, but rather
because they lived with the Spaniards and praised them or defended those whom everyone
so hated, or perhaps because those Indians had done them some harm under orders to the
Spaniards, as we have so very often seen. And in these cases, God had great mercy upon
them if they were saved because they confessed themselves his servants. I always gathered
and understood that the peoples of the neighboring islands had the same kind of religion
as that of this Island of Hispaniola, but they did not have very consequential idols, nor did
they offer them sacrifices excepting those fasts and a certain part of the grain they harvested, as will be seen below when we discuss sacrifices, nor any other ceremonies excepting
those *cohobas* with which they intoxicated themselves. And as I have always understood,
the purest of all in this matter were the very simple people of the Bahamas, whom I have
many times above compared to the people of Serica [silk growers of the Far East], happy
nation. We do not believe these people had any sign of idolatry or evil belief or external
figure or image; on the contrary, we believe that they lived simply with the universal and
confused knowledge of a first cause, which is God, and that he dwelt in the heavens."

it will be appropriate to relate the sacrifices of these our new nations, which we commonly call the Indies.

And beginning, as always, with this Island of Hispaniola, great island, I say the following: that in accordance with the knowledge that men and nations achieved and today achieve of God, so do they serve, honor, and worship him, building temples to him, priests, ceremonies, and sacrifices, for all this is based, proceeds, and is derived from the first issue, which is the knowledge, as has been seen from all the nearly infinite number of reasons and examples we have given with such great discourse. The peoples of this island and all those of its surroundings had a meager, weak, and confused knowledge of God, although more pure or less dirty in the horrors of idolatry than many others; hence, it was that they had neither idols nor many gods, excepting a few or almost none, nor temples nor priests, excepting very few or almost none, only those whom above we called soothsayers and physicians, and as a result, there were very few sacrifices, although they had some. Of these I will relate what I know and saw and what others experienced.

We found that in the season when they gathered the harvest of the fields they had sown and cultivated, which consisted of the bread made from roots, the yams, sweet potatoes, and corn, they donated a certain portion as first fruits, almost as if they were giving thanks for benefits received. Because they had no designated temples or houses of religion, as has been said above, they put this portion or first fruits of the crops in the great house of the lords and *caciques,* which they called *caney,* and they offered and dedicated it to the zemi. They said the zemi sent the water and brought the sun and nurtured all those fruits and gave them children and the other benefits that were there in abundance. All the things offered in this way were left there either until they rotted or the children took them or played with them or until they were spoiled, and thus they were consumed.

Before New Spain and the provinces of Naco, Honduras, and Peru were discovered, when I saw how the Indians of these islands, particularly Hispaniola and Cuba, took such care to give this portion of the fruits they gathered as first fruits and to use them as offerings in that way, I began to notice that the duty to make sacrifice to God was a natural law, something that I had read but not seen before. Saint Thomas proves this in the *Secunda secundae,* question 85, first article, which says as follows: "Oblatio sacrificiorum pertinent ad jus naturale," etc. And it was said above, as a maxim of Porphyry, that all the ancients offered the first fruits. Something all men do without being taught and are inclined to do of their own volition presents a clear argument for its being a natural law, as was also stated above regarding these natural inclinations in chapter . . . something. When I would ask the Indians at times: "Who is this zemi you name?" they answered me: "He who makes it rain and makes the sun shine and gives us children and the other benefits we desire." I added: "May the zemi who does that take my soul." Here I took the occasion to preach something about God to them, although in those days (I say it to my consternation) God had not yet shown me the great mercy he did later when he gave me knowledge of the necessities these people suffered in their temporal and spiritual health, there being in them the disposition to be brought to Jesus Christ very quickly and admirably, and also when he led me to understand that we Christians who come to these lands have a strict obligation to succor our so needy fellow men. From what I have said, it seems to follow that the peoples of these islands have a knowledge, although confused, of one God, as we have discussed above.

We already said above in chapter . . . how on this island they had certain statues, although few of them; it is believed the devil spoke in these statues to the priests, who were called *behicos,* and also to the lords or kings when they were so disposed, so that those statues were their oracles. For this purpose they had another sacrifice and ceremonies that they practiced so as to please the statue, which he must have taught them. This was done as follows: they made certain powders from certain very dry and well-ground herbs that were like cinnamon or ground henna in color; in short, they were tawny colored. These powders were put in a round dish, not flat but rather a little curved or deep, made of such beautiful, smooth, and pretty wood that it would not have been much more beautiful had it been made of gold or silver; it was almost black and shone like jet. They had an instrument made of the same wood and material and with the same sheen and beauty; that instrument was constructed the size of a small flute, completely hollow as is the flute, and two-thirds of the way down it separated into two hollow tubes, in the way we separate the two middle fingers, with the thumb held back, when we extend a hand. They placed those two tubes into both nostrils and the top of the flute, so to speak, in the powder on the dish, and they inhaled; as they inhaled, they took in through their nostrils the dose of powder they had decided to consume. When they had consumed it, they immediately went out of their minds, and it was almost as if they had drunk a great deal of strong wine, whereby they ended up inebriated or almost so. These powders and these ceremonies or acts were called *co-*

hoba, the middle syllable long in their language. They spoke there as if in gibberish or like Germans, confusedly, I know not what words and things. Then they were worthy of the colloquy with the statues and oracles, or more properly speaking, with the enemy of human nature; in this manner, the secrets were revealed to them, and they prophesied or foretold. They heard and learned in this way if some good, adversity, or harm was to come to them.

This was when the priest alone made ready to speak and for the statue to speak to him. But when all the leaders of the people gathered to make that sacrifice (which they called *cohoba*), whether they were persuaded by the *behiques* or priests, or by the lords, then it was amazing to see them. In order to hold their councils or to decide difficult matters, such as if they ought to press forward in one of their little wars or to undertake some other matters that seemed important to them, their custom was to make their *cohoba* and in that way to intoxicate themselves or nearly.

This manner of deliberation, very full of wine and inebriated or nearly, was not original with these people; according to Herodotus in book 1 and Strabo at the end of book 15, the Persians practiced this method when there were matters of weight and great import to deliberate. They never deliberated except while they were eating and drinking, and they were well filled with wine, and they said that such councils and the decisions that emerged from them were more enduring than decisions made in sobriety and temperance.

I saw them celebrate their *cohoba* a few times, and it was something to see how they took it and what they said. The first to begin was the lord, and while he took it, everyone kept silent; when he had taken his *cohoba* (which is to inhale those powders through the nostrils, as has been said), and they took it seated on some low but very well-carved benches that they called *duohos* (the first syllable long), he would stay awhile with his head turned to one side and his arms placed on his knees, and afterwards he would lift his face toward heaven and speak his certain words, which must have been his prayer to the true God or to the one whom he held to be a god; then everyone would respond almost like when we respond "Amen," and they would do this with a great clamor of voices or sounds, and then they would give thanks to him, and they must have flattered him with praises, winning his benevolence and begging him to tell what he had seen. He would give them an account of his vision, saying that the zemi had spoken and assured him of good or adverse times, or that there were to be children, or that there was to be a death among them, or that they were to have some contention or war with their neighbors, and other foolishness that came to their imagination, stirred up by that intoxication or that the devil, perhaps, and haplessly had insinuated to them so as to deceive them and inculcate in them a devotion to him.

They had a thousand tall tales, apparently like the fables feigned by the poets among the ancient Greeks and Romans, although in many of their fictions, but not in all, the poets sought to include allegories and some morality so as to induce men to adopt good customs; we do not know what these people meant to understand or to signify in their fantasies. Like the stories they told about the zemi of Buyayba (which was, I believe, a village), they said the zemi they called Vaybrama, the penultimate syllable long, had been burned in a war they had waged, and when they washed him with the juice of the root we said above was called *yuca* [cassava], from which they made cassava bread, he grew arms, and his eyes reappeared, and his body grew; and because *yuca* or the aforesaid root was very small in those days, after they washed him with *yuca* water, it was henceforth, as it now is, fat and very large. This zemi brought diseases to men, according to their belief, for which they sought the help of the priests or *behiques,* who were their prophets and theologians as has been said; these priests would respond that the disease had befallen them because they had been negligent or forgetful in bringing cassava bread and yams and other things to eat to the ministers who swept and cleaned the house or hermitage of Vaybrama, good zemi, and that he had told him so.

Those *behiques* told them many other fictions and tales; unless they were meant to signify some allegory or morality, like the ancient poets, they were inventions of the devil or great nonsense.

CHAPTER CLXVII

Concerning the fasts kept by the Indians of the Island
of Hispaniola and of Cuba in honor of their idols
They also had another sacrifice, rite or manner of worship, and this was a great fast, and they began it in this way: the friar Fray Ramón, whom we mentioned above when we spoke of the gods of this island and who came here five years before me, tells that on this island there was the renown and belief that a certain *cacique* and king of theirs made a certain abstinence to the Great Lord who lives in the heaven, whence others' knowledge and opinion of a God in heaven must have been derived. The abstinence was that they retreated for six or seven days without eating anything except certain juices of herbs so as not to weaken altogether, with which juice they also washed their bodies; those herbs must have

had some power, like the herb from Peru they call coca and the others that Pliny discusses and in chapter . . . we made mention of them. During that fast, because their heads were feeble, there came or appeared to them certain shapes or fantasies of what they wanted to know or, what is more to be believed, that the devil put into their minds and depicted to deceive them. Although the first *cacique* or lord or lords who invented or began that fast and abstinence did it out of devotion to the Lord who is in heaven, and he wanted or meant to request of him that the Lord speak to him or respond to what he wished; those who afterwards continued to fast must have done it in honor of the zemis, or idols or statues, or the one who endeavored with those statues to lead them astray from the knowledge of the true God and who, little by little, always gained something from them in this case because, as has been said many times, they were lacking grace and doctrine.

This can be argued because of what those of us who were first on the island of Cuba learned of its inhabitants and the ceremony they practiced. On that island the fast held by some, principally the *behiques* or priests or soothsayers, was strange and frightening. They would fast for four months and more at one stretch, without eating anything except only a certain juice of an herb or herbs that sufficed only to sustain their life and keep them from dying; hence, one can deduce that the power of that herb or herbs must have been very great, much greater than those of which Pliny speaks in book 25, chapter 8, and to which we refer above. And this is the same coca that is so esteemed in the provinces of Peru, as we know from the testimony of the clerics and the Indians who have come from Peru, who saw it and first became acquainted with it on the aforesaid Island of Cuba and in great abundance. When they were enfeebled, thus, and tormented by that cruel and very harsh and extended fast, for they came within a hairbreadth of dying, they were then prepared and worthy, it was said, for the zemi to appear to them and to see his face, which could not have been other than the devil's. Then he answered and informed them regarding what they were asking, and whatever else he added to deceive them, all of which the *behiques* later reported and affirmed to the other people. There was on the Island of Cuba only this indication and deception of idolatry and no other that we perceived because we found neither idols nor statue nor any other thing that smacked of idolatry.

And this seems a marvelous business, that fasting and abstinence should be of such power that they are agreeable even to the devil, that the devil should require of his servants such a daily injury to the flesh, and that only those people whose senses were mortified and nearly dead should be able to see his infernal presence because the devil takes more pleasure in the inebriation and gluttony of his people because these are the fountain and mother from which all vices spring, according to Saint Crisostomo, chapter 27, homily 58 about Saint Matthew, and the virtue of fasting is one of the arms with which they are to be defeated, as the Savior advised: "Hoc genus daemoniorum non ejicitur nisi in oratione et jejunio" (Mataei, chapter 17). But the devil urged or ordered this fast and abstinence only because of his very ancient and overweening pride, which drove him to wish to usurp that virtue, as the honor and worship pertaining to God, not because it was a virtue, but because by requesting it he sought to make men understand that he loved virtue and thereby to increase his credibility with them. He did so also to offend and torment their bodies in this life, as their souls in the other life, with that harsh and fruitless injury because of the hate he harbors for men; thus he always enjoys their torments and travails, inflicting upon them his deep cruelty.

Returning to the subject of the *cacique* or lord who had begun that fast, they said and it was public knowledge that when he spoke with a certain zemi whose name was Yocahuguamá, the zemi had told him that those who were alive after his death would enjoy his lands and house little time because a clothed people would come who would conquer and kill them, and they would die of hunger. Thenceforward, they believed those people must have been those whom we call Caribs, and at that time they called them and we called them cannibals. All this Fray Ramón says he has understood from the Indians. He says some other things that are confused and of little substance, as a simple person who did not speak our Castilian tongue altogether well because he was a Catalan by birth, and therefore it is better not to relate these things. I want only to tell what he affirms about an Indian or Indians whom he converted to Christianity. When other Indians were killing them because of the hate they had for the Spaniards, they cried in a loud voice: "Dios naboría daca, Dios naboría daca," which means in the most common and universal language of this island, "I am a servant of God"; this man was called Juan, and in this manner and speaking these words, another man died called Antón, who was his brother. *Naboría* meant "servant or manservant," and *daca* means "I." And thus Fray Ramón said these men were martyrs, about which no Christian can harbor any doubt if they were killed for their faith or for refusing to relinquish their faith or for some other virtue. But they did not kill them for that reason because no Indian ever did such a thing, but rather because they lived with the Spaniards and praised them or defended those whom everyone so hated, or because perhaps those Indians had done them some harm under orders from the Spaniards, as we have so very often seen. And in these cases God had great mercy upon them if they were saved because they confessed themselves his servants, but not because they were martyrs.

I always gathered and understood that the peoples of the neighboring islands had the same kind of religion as that of this Island of Hispaniola, but they did not have very consequential idols (we found none on the Island of Cuba), nor did they offer them sacrifices excepting those fasts and a certain part of the grain they harvested, nor any other ceremonies excepting those *cohobas* with which they nearly intoxicated themselves. And as I have always understood, the purest of all in this matter were the very simple people of the Bahamas, whom I have many times above compared to the people of Serica [silk growers of the Far East], happy nation. We do not believe these people had any sign of idolatry or evil belief or external figure or image or statue; on the contrary, we believe they lived simply with the universal and confused knowledge of a first cause, which is God, and that he dwelt in the heavens, and thus we have no reason to stop to relate their sacrifices.

Fernando's *Historia,* and therefore Pané's *Relación,* has had a wide circulation in translation in English, French, and other languages. In keeping with the purpose of the project at hand, however, I will limit this bibliographic note to the first edition of the Italian version prepared by Ulloa (because all the other editions and translations, directly or indirectly, derive from it) and to the major retranslations of Pané's booklet into Spanish.

The copy of the first edition I have used is located in the Rare Book Section of the Yale University Library. Its title reads:

> Historie Del S. D. Fernando Colo[mbo:] Nelle quali s'ha particolare, & vera relatio[ne] della vita, & de'fatti dell'Ammiraglio D. Christoforo Colombo, suo padre. Et dello scoprimento, ch'egli feci dell'Indie Occidentali, dette Mondo Nvovo, hora possedute dal Sereniss. Re Catolico: Nuouamente di lingua Spagnuola tradotte nell'Italiana dal S. Alfonso Vlloa. In Venetia, MDLXXI. Appresso Francesco de'Franceschi Sanese.

The copy consists of nineteen preliminary pages, 247 numbered folios, and measures fifteen-by-ten centimeters. The *Relación* occupies folios 126v to 145v and carries the following title:

> Scritvra di fra Roman delle antichità de gli'Indiani, le quali egli con diligenza, come huomo che sà la lor lingua, ha raccolte per commandamento dello Ambiraglio.

Because doubts have arisen as to whether this is the first edition or not, a brief digression here is worthwhile to resolve the matter definitively. Given the constant interest in Colombine matters, numerous reeditions of Ulloa's translation have been published in Italy: I know of at least four from the seventeenth century (in Milano, Apresso Girolamo Bordoni, 1614; in Venetia, Apresso Gio. Pietro Brigonci, 1676; in Venetia, Apresso Iseppo Prodocimo, 1678; in Venetia, Apresso Giuseppe Tramontin, 1685), two from the eighteenth century (in Venetia, Per il Prodocimo, 1709; in Venetia, Per il Lovisa, 1728), and several more from the nineteenth and twentieth centuries. Of those versions, the one published in Venice by Prodocimo in 1709 demands particular attention. I have seen two copies of that edition: one in Yale and the other in Princeton. In the Princeton Library copy, the year of publication has been scratched out, on both the title page and the dedication, and the date 1569 has been printed over the scratching. Those alterations, made perhaps in more than one copy, have given cause for some scholars to believe that the first edition dates from 1569. In fact, it is a question of a clumsy fraud. A comparison of both copies reveals that they agree exactly in the design of the title page, the size of the case, the numeration of the pages, the types of letters and even the omissions and frequent errors that make this edition one of the most corrupt of all.

There are three major Spanish translations. The first appeared in volume 1 of *Historiadores primitivos de las Indias Occidentales, que juntó, traduxo en parte, y sacó a luz, ilustrados con eruditas notas, y copiosos índices, el ilustrísimo señor D. Andrés González Barcia* (Madrid, 1749). The title of Fernando's work reads as follows:

> La historia de D. Fernando Colón en la cual se da particular, y verdadera relación de la vida, y hechos de el almirante D. Christóval Colón, su padre, y del descubrimiento de las Indias Occidentales, llamadas Nuevo Mundo, que pertenece al Serenísimo Rei de España, que tradujo de español en italiano Alonso de Ulloa; y aora, por no parecer el original español, sacada del traslado italiano.

Pané's booklet occupies pages 62 to 71, and its title was translated thus:

> Escritura de Fr. Román, del Orden de San Gerónimo. De la Antiguedad de los Indios, la qual, como sugeto, que sabe su lengua, recogió con diligencia, de orden del Almirante.

I have information that this version was reprinted in Buenos Aires in 1844, but I have not seen a copy of it. It was also reprinted by José María Asensio in the second volume of his *Cristóbal Colón, su vida . . .* (Barcelona, 1891), pages 123–38. And it appeared as well in the *Colección de libros raros o curioos que tratan de América*, volumes 5 and 6 (Madrid, 1892).

The second important retranslation was by Manuel Serrano y Sanz. This version appeared with the title, *Historia del almirante don Cristóbal Colón, por su hijo Hernando: traducida nuevamente del italiano . . .* (Madrid, Librería General de Victoriano Suárez, 1932). It consists of two volumes. Pané's booklet occupies pages [35] to 90 of volume 2, and its title reads:

Relación de fray Ramón acerca de las antigüedades de los indios, las cuales, con diligencia, como hombre que sabe el idioma de éstos, recogió por mandato del Almirante.

In the most recent of the retranslations into Spanish, a different title has been chosen, relieved of annoying details. This edition, perhaps the most abbreviated and accessible of the three, is the following: *Vida del almirante don Cristóbal Colón escrita por su hijo Hernando Colón* (Mexico, Fondo de Cultura Económica, 1947). Pané's account appears on pages 186 to 206, and its heading reads thus:

Relación de Fray Ramón acerca de las antigüedades de los indios, las cuales, con diligencias, como hombre que sabe su idioma, recogió por mandato del Almirante.

From Pané's account alone, independent translations and editions have also been made. Of these I have seen four: three done in the Antilles and one in Buenos Aires. The earliest is that which Antonio Bachiller y Morales inserted into his work *Cuba primitiva: Origen, lenguas, tradiciones e historia de los Indios de las Antillas Mayores y las Lucayas*, second edition revised and expanded (Havana, 1883), pp. 165-83. To Bachiller belongs the distinction of having been the first to recognize the need to correct the deformations that had distorted the Taíno words. Because he did not locate the first edition and he lacked some scholarly tools of evidence that have since appeared, his efforts did not achieve the success they deserved. He left, however, a clear definition of the problem.

In the twentieth century, the expansion of the study of American mythologies has facilitated the publication of other versions of Pané's account. The first of these appeared, as indicated by Fernando Ortiz, in the journal *Archivos del Folklore Cubano* 1, no. 2 (1924). Luis Florén Lozano published, with a brief introduction, "La Relación de la antigüedad de los Indios de la Española de Fray Román Pané" in the *Anales de la Universidad de Santo Domingo* 12 (1947): 109-38. And it has also circulated in a separate little volume under a new title, although this new title was doubly ill-advised because it obscures the content of the work and affirms an incorrect date: *Relación de Indias 1496; prólogo y notas por Alberto Wildner-Fox* (Buenos Aires, 1954). These publications belong, thus, to a long tradition. The present volume joins them in the hope that it may contribute to the resolution of some of the difficulties indicated by Bachiller y Morales.

INDEX OF TAÍNO WORDS AND NAMES

The terms listed here are given just as they appear in the text of the current edition. Variants found in Ulloa, Pietro Martire, Las Casas, or other sources are indicated in the notes to the text. When a variant differs to such an extent that it may be difficult to locate in this index, it is included in parentheses following the chosen spelling or is listed, in alphabetical order, with a reference to the form deemed more appropriate.

José Juan Arrom, editor of this volume, is professor emeritus of Latin American literature, Department of Spanish and Portuguese, Yale University. He is the author and editor of many works, including *El teatro de Hispanoamérica en la época colonial* (1967); *Esquema generacional de las letras hispano-americanas: ensayo de un método* (1977); and *Imaginación del Nuevo Mundo: Diez estudios sobre los inicios de la narrativa hispanoamericana* (1991).

Library of Congress Cataloging-in-Publication Data
Pané, Ramón.
[Relación acerca de las antigüedades de los indios. English]
An account of the antiquities of the Indians : chronicles of the New World encounter / Ramón Pané. — A new ed. / introductory study, notes, and appendixes by José Juan Arrom ; translated by Susan C. Griswold
    p.   cm. — (Latin America in translation/en traducción/ en tradução)
Includes bibliographical references.
ISBN 0-8223-2325-7 (alk. paper). — ISBN 0-8223-2347-8 (pbk.: alk. paper)
1. Indians of the West Indies—Hispaniola—History—Sources.
2. Indians of the West Indies—Hispaniola—First contact with Europeans.   3. Indians of the West Indies—Hispaniola— Religion.   4. Hispaniola—History—Sources.   I. Arrom, José Juan, 1910- .   II. Title.   III. Series.
F1909.P3613   1999
972.93—dc21   99-19365